PAT O'BRYAN

THE ABSOLUTE BEGINNER'S GUIDE TO INTERNET WEALTH

**EVERYTHING You NEED TO KNOW
to Create Your Portable Empire**

NEW YORK

THE ABSOLUTE BEGINNER'S GUIDE TO INTERNET WEALTH

Copyright ©2007 Pat O'Bryan

ISBN: 978-1-60037-030-4 (Paperback)
ISBN: 978-1-60037-191-2 (Hardcover)
ISBN: 978-1-60037-031-1 (Audio)
ISBN: 978-1-60037-192-9 (eBook)

Published by:

MORGAN · JAMES
THE ENTREPRENEURIAL PUBLISHER™
www.morganjamespublishing.com

Morgan James Publishing, LLC
1225 Franklin Ave Ste 32
Garden City, NY 11530-1693
Toll Free 800-485-4943
www.MorganJamesPublishing.com

Cover/Interior Design by:
Rachel Campbell
rcampbell77@cox.net

Please write *Pat@PatOBryan.com*, or contact Pat O'Bryan, The Milagro Research Institute, P. O. Box 2272, Wimberley, Texas 78676.

TABLE OF CONTENTS

Foreword	**vii**
Author's Foreword	**ix**

Getting Started- Choosing Your Niche	1
How to Create Valuable Information Products Automatically	9
Why Write An eBook?	11
What To Write about	13
The Public Domain	15
Find a Work in the Public Domain	17
Rebrand a Public Domain Work	19
Chapter Review – Rebrand a Public Domain Book	*21*
Write a Workbook or Study Guide Using a Public Domain Work	23
Chapter Review – Write A Workbook or Study Guide	*25*
Get Others To Write Your eBook For You.	27
Chapter Review – Get Others To Write Your eBook For You	*29*
Use Interviews To Write An eBook	31
Chapter Review – Using Interviews To Write An eBook	*37*
Use Search Engines to Write Your eBook	39

Chapter Review – Using Search Engines to Write Your eBook   41

Use Lists to Write Your eBook   43

Chapter Review – Using Lists to Write Your eBook   45

What _____ Can Teach Us about _____.   47

Chapter Review – What _____ Can Teach Us about _____.   49

Now What?   51

The Absolute Beginner's Guide to Copywriting   53

The Basics   55

The Headline   57

The Question   59

The Call-Out   61

A Little Psychology   63

Imagine That…   65

Quotes-   67

Steal This Ad   69

Bullet Points   71

Sub-Heads   75

The Body   77

Testimonials   81

The Guarantee   83

The Close   85

The P.S.   87

What To Do Next   89

The Absolute Beginner's Guide to Joint Venture Proposals   91

Why Joint Venture?   93

Lists   95

Who Is Your Customer?   97

Types of Joint Venture Partners   99

Stalking the 800-Pound Gorilla   101

The Big Dogs   105

Everybody Else   107

What about the Competition?   109

Sample Joint Venture Letter   111

Go To Work!   113

SEO FOR BEGINNERS   115

INTRODUCTION: WHAT IS SEARCH ENGINE OPTIMIZATION?   117

Part I. Creating A Search Engine Friendly Web Page   121

  2. How Free Hosting Can Cost You   127

    Speed and Reliability   127

    Subdomains   128

  2. What's In a Domain Name?   129

    Plurals, "The", and "My" Forms of the Domain Name   132

    How to Register a Domain Name   135

    Step-By-Step Instructions   135

Part II. Using SEO Content To Create A Web Presence   137

  1. What's In A Title?   137

  2. The Art of the Blurb   138

  3. Writing Search Engine Optimized Content   139

  4. How To Choose the Right Keywords   140

  5. Use Articles and Information as Traffic Magnets   141

  6. Buying Articles From Syndication Sites   142

  7. Pay For Premium Content   143

  8. Hire A Ghost Writer   143

  9. Get Your Visitors to Supply Your Content   144

  10. Make Them Sign a Guestbook   144

11. Add a Section of Useful Links   145

12. Add a Forum, Blog or Chat Room   145

13. Add a "Recommend Your Site Function"   146

14. Install a Search Engine   146

Part III. Submitting Your Site to the Search Engines   *147*

1. A Simple Plan of Action   147

2. Determine Your Keyphrases   149

3. Creating a Title Tag   150

4. Mastering Meta Tags   151

5. The Keyword Blurb   154

6. Submitting to the Big Indexes   154

   Yahoo!   155

   How to Apply to Yahoo!   157

   The Open Directory Project   159

   About.com   159

7. How To Be Ignored By The Search Engines   160

8. Free Online Keyword Tools   161

9. Five Tips Before You Submit   163

About the Author   **167**

FOREWORD

DR. JOE VITALE

Can anyone – even you – make money online?

Before you answer, consider the following:

I started as an Internet skeptic over 15 years ago. I thought the rumors of gold in cyberspace were hype. As usual, I was wrong. I'm living proof. I went from nothing online to being something of a cyberspace celebrity. Google my name and look out. I've got more websites than most people have time to review. I've got more books online that most people read in a lifetime, and the best news of all is that they all make me money, even while I sleep...

...even while I write this foreword.

Maybe you think I'm an exception.

So, you're a skeptic, too?

Well, look at the author of this very book. He was a successful musician. By "successful" I mean he had CDs out, he was performing, and people were applauding.

But he was broke.

I still remember the day he came to my house, red faced in frustration, saying he just wanted to make enough money to pay his fricking rent.

Today he is an Internet guru in his own right. He pays his rent just fine. I've seen him splurge on new cars, guitars (including one for me), gadgets and gifts, trips, and more. He learned quickly, took action, and kept cranking out new products. Given that the Internet is a marvelous place to try ideas for virtually nothing, he was able to get up and running almost overnight. Today he's a success, and he's written this book.

You can do this, too.

How?

This book explains it all, step by step. The beautiful thing about the author is that he is articulate, colorful, memorable and caring. He takes his time to be sure you understand the online world. He takes you by the hand and teaches you, from the kindergarten stage on up, how to make money online. Whether you're a newbie or a seasoned nettie, you'll learn from this book.

I'm flattered that Pat asked me to write this introduction for you, but I'm more proud of his success. If he can go from zero to $100,000 in one month, and if I can begin as a skeptic and make a name for myself online, think of what is possible for you. We didn't have this book when we started. You do. You have the edge.

I will be watching for your smoke.

Go for it.

Dr. Joe Vitale
Author of way too many books to list here
See *www.MrFire.com*

AUTHOR'S FOREWORD

It's late August, 2006, as I write this.

Looking back, it seems a blur. Like Joe says in his Foreword, two and a half years ago, I was a broke blues guitarist. It looked romantic from the outside, I've been told – European tours, recording and publishing deals, transcontinental semi-stardom – but the reality was just a puff of smoke above poverty: one night stands, really cheap hotels, and miles and miles of windshield time.

Worse, it was a treadmill. I was trading my time for money. I was either thousands of miles from my family, driving from gig to gig, or I was unemployed.

In Wimberley, between tours, I would meet my friend Bill Hibbler (*www.eCommerceConfidential.com*), another Rock and Roll survivor, for coffee. I'd tell him about the months of one-night stands, drunken fans, and chump change. He'd tell me about his current eBook, affiliate campaign, or list-building strategy.

At first, I listened politely. After a while, I took a little more notice. Bill was making a lot more money than I was, and it seemed like he was hardly working at all. Even more interestingly, he was creating streams of passive income. Once I "got" that concept, I was hooked.

In 2003, Bill introduced me to Joe. When Joe found out that I was a blues guitarist, and had played with some of his guitar-god heroes, like Stevie Ray Vaughan, B.B. King, and Johnny Winter, he asked me what I'd charge for guitar lessons.

In an uncharacteristically lucid moment, I said, "I'll trade you guitar lessons for marketing lessons." With completely characteristic grace, Joe took that deal.

This ranks with the beads for real-estate acquisition of Manhattan and the Louisiana Purchase in the universe of great deals- for me. I still owe Joe a lot of guitar lessons.

If I had to describe the secret of my success, I'd say it was that I listened closely when Joe talked, and when he said a book was worth reading, I read it, and I took action.

Joe says this book is worth reading. The action part is up to you.

Of course, as time went on, I met other gurus – mostly through Joe and Bill. I'm very grateful to them.

In 2004, Joe hosted a seminar in Austin, and gave Bill and me complementary tickets. Of course, we made the hour drive to Austin each day. Rooms in a nice hotel were way out of my reach.

That's where I met Craig Perrine (*www.MaverickMarketer.com*), who has patiently guided me in my list-building success, for which I am very grateful every time I email my list. If there's a funnier Internet marketer out there, I haven't met them.

One of the speakers at that seminar was Cindy Cashman (*www.First-SpaceWedding.com*). Cindy, Craig, Bill and I are all now members of the same MasterMind group, along with Joe (*www.MrFire.com*), Nerissa Oden (*www.TheVideoQueen.com*) and Jillian Coleman Wheeler (*www.GrantM-eRich.com*). Over time, I came to realize that Cindy was one of the most brilliant and inspirational humans in the Galaxy. She made her first million dollars with a blank book. She's going to be the first woman to get married in outer-space. She swims with dolphins and stands on her head for fun. Just knowing she exists makes me smile.

After a while, I started attending Internet marketing seminars, where I met Armand Morin, David Garfinkel, Dave Lakhani, Declan Dunn, Frank Garon, and others. They've all gracefully provided valuable pieces to the puzzle.

Fast forward to today.

I'm running a Portable Empire™.

My eBooks and audio products are all over the 'net, and selling like hotcakes. My "Your Portable Empire" un-seminars (*www.YourPortableEmpire.com*) are selling out, at $997 per seat. My video production company is building a phenomenal library of educational videos, and we sold over $100,000 of them last month. My mentoring program is hatching a new crop of Internet pro's regularly (*www.PatOBryan.com/mentor.htm*).

The future's so bright, I gotta wear shades.

Two and a half years ago, when I was first blindly feeling my way around, trying to get a grasp on the slippery subject of Internet marketing, I would have committed a serious felony to get my hands on a book that explained the basics in simple terms that even I could understand.

I wanted a book that laid out a simple path from "nowhere" to "Internet wealth."

If such a book existed, I couldn't find it.

This is that book.

There really is a formula for online success. You need a list of people who are interested in your topic. You need to develop a relationship with the humans on that list. You need products to sell them.

There are many other things you can do to increase your online wealth, but until you've mastered the basics, those are just distractions.

So, here's *The Absolute Beginners Guide to Online Wealth*.

With this book, and the gumption to take action and put its concepts into practice, you should be able to create your own Portable Empire™ quickly.

Enjoy-

Pat O'Bryan

August 26, 2006

CHAPTER 1

GETTING STARTED – CHOOSING YOUR NICHE

here are three main components to keep in mind when you're building your Portable Empire:

1. **Building your list**
2. **Building your relationship with your list**
3. **Making products and selling them to your list, and through Joint Venture and affiliate arrangements, to the universe.**

Let's talk about choosing your niche. This is the playground where you're going to play- so keep it interesting and fun.

According to the Merriam-Webster dictionary, niche means:

> 2 a : a place, employment, status, or activity for which a person or thing is best fitted <finally found her *niche*> b : a habitat supplying the factors necessary for the existence of an organism or species c : the ecological role of an organism in a community especially in regard to food consumption d : a specialized market

When we talk about our "niche" in Internet marketing, we're referring to "d: a specialized market," although the other definitions are relevant.

It's important to target all of your efforts to one specific, specialized market. To develop a large, loyal list of subscribers, you need to offer a solution to a problem that is shared by a large group of people.

Over time, one of your most valuable possessions will be your list of people who are not only interested in the solution to their problem, but will also pay you for solutions.

If you choose your niche wisely, it will be deep enough to include a lot of related problems. For example, my niche is education, specifically in the area of Internet marketing for beginners.

That's a big playground. I can talk about the mindset of success, the inner game of marketing, how to create a PDF file, video editing, and hundreds of other related topics. I can provide the information as an eBook, an audio download, a CD, a streaming video, or a DVD.

You might want to jot this down: "Every problem is a product."

As my customer solves one problem – hopefully with a solution they buy from me – which leads them to the next problem. My job is to make sure they know about the problem, and make it easy for them to buy the solution from me. At that point, the client will weigh how important the problem is to them, how long it would take them to solve it on their own, and hopefully, purchase the solution.

Over time, I've created a lot of solutions. As I solve each problem for myself, I turn that solution into a product.

To the people who are behind us on the learning curve, we're the experts.

Over time, I've left a trail of solutions, and gathered a list of people who are on the same journey as I am. This is how you create multiple streams of passive income.

As you read the instructions below for choosing a niche, keep that in mind. Be sure to pick a niche that has a long learning curve, with lots of fun problems.

Let's take this to the real world.

One of the best tools for communicating with your subscribers is a blog (web log). I advertise mine as "unedited and uncensored," and do my best to keep it real and relevant, with tongue planted firmly in cheek.

Here's an excerpt from my blog (*www.PatOBryan.com/blog.htm*):

Recently, one of my mentoring clients asked:

> **Could you please explain how you coach people to success? I have been down this road before trying to come up with a product to solve a problem. I didn't come up with anything! I don't have a clue when coming up with a product... Do you have a specific process to come up with profitable ideas??? I hope so, I need the process you go thru.**

I responded:

I suspect that he's not the only one asking this question. As a matter of fact, my domestic partner, Betsy and I were just talking about this over dinner. She's struggling with the same problem.

I think we can sort this out.

First, you need to chunk the question down and simplify it. Right now, the problem I'd like to solve is breast cancer – a very dear friend is battling this demon, and I've lost several loved ones to it. Another problem I'd like solved is political - I'm afraid that Ike was right when he warned us to beware the military-industrial complex. Then there's hunger, homelessness, global warming, and the fact that there's not a real first-class Mexican Food restaurant in Wimberley, Texas.

Realistically, I'm not an oncologist, a political scientist, social scientist, or first-class Mexican Food chef. We need to find problems we can actually solve, and hopefully in a niche that we can stay interested in.

To me, that's the real danger – finding a niche that's profitable but boring. I think it's important to find a niche about which you're passionate.

For example, I'm passionate about self-actualization, and I don't think that's something you can achieve working 40 hours a week at a job you don't love. I think humans were created in God's image, and He didn't intend for us to spend our brief time on this spinning globe in mind-numbing tedium. I'm convinced that we're living in an infinite universe, and that there are enough resources for everyone. My solution is the "Portable Empire" concept, which allows you to travel, think, meditate, and grow to your full potential without having to punch a clock.

When I'm looking for a problem to solve, I limit my search to the niche of "Your Portable Empire."

That simplifies the problem, and also simplifies finding the solution. I promote seminars, videos, audios and eBooks that teach people to create multiple streams of passive income.

A lot of my products start out as conversations with my mentoring clients. Step one is to identify your niche.

How do you do that? You need to find a subject that you're a) passionate about, b) knowledgeable in, and c) is broad enough to have a large customer base.

In my case, I'm passionate about freedom – and you need financial freedom to acquire intellectual freedom and freedom of mobility. I'm knowledgeable about the subject – I make a healthy six-figure income doing what

I teach, and finally, there are more than enough people interested in the subject to make it profitable for me.

One way to work your way through the niche-finding problem is to take a piece of paper and draw a line down the middle. On one side, write down all the subjects you're knowledgeable about. An example could be:

Raising Happy Children

Maintaining Automobiles

Losing Weight

Yoga

Golf

Healthy Relationships

Feng Shui

Getting a Good Deal on Antiques

Graphic Design

Cleaning Houses

Cooking

Art (painting, drawing, collecting, et cetera)

Music (playing an instrument, promoting a band, making a recording, et cetera)

Poker

Chess

Stock Market Investing

Take some time with this – you know a lot more than you think you do. Then, in the second column, make a similar list of things you're passionate about. PASSIONATE! Not just interested.

Then, see what turns up in both columns. On another sheet of paper, make another list of just the things that are in both columns, with the most fascinating (to you) subject first, the next most fascinating subject second, et cetera.

Now, starting with the most interesting subject, do a Google search to see who else is marketing to your future customers.

If you turn up a blank, or just a few results, go to the next one. Just because you're passionate about under-water stamp collecting doesn't mean it's a good business model. Call that a hobby and move on.

If your Google search turns up page after page of commercial sites-congratulations! You've just identified your future Joint Venture partners. You've found your niche.

Now, let's say you're the kind of guy who plays 18 holes of golf every morning, and another 18 in the evening. You've got zirconium encrusted drivers and a putter that's been blessed by three popes. Your golf cart has a hemi. Your wife would like you to kindly shut up about golf, because that's all you ever talk about.

You're a golf nut.

Now, let's also postulate that you've spent a few years reading every book you can get your hands on about golf, studied with Tiger Woods, and the local golf pro asks you for advice.

You're a golf expert.

You do a Google search on "golf" and discover that there are thousands of people marketing to golfers.

You're in luck.

Your niche is golf.

Now, to monetize your niche, you need to find out what pressing problems golfers are having and provide them with a solution. You want to identify a problem that really, really hurts them. I live on a golf course, but the last golf course I played on had a windmill, and I was still in Junior High School at the time, so I'm going to wing it here...

Do they slice? Do they get tired on hole 17? Hole 3? Is their stance too wide? Are their pants too tight? Have they lost their balls?

How do you find out what THE pressing problem is for golfers today?

Back to Google!

Do a search on "golf forum."

There should be plenty. Join them. Lurk. Read the posts.

I do this with "newbie" Internet forums. It's a gold mine. Somebody will post a question, several other people will join the conversation, mentioning that they've had the same problem. Somebody will post a wrong answer.

Gold mine. Home run. Hole in one.

So, hang out in the forums and identify the one biggest problem that golfers have. Obviously, this will work in any niche.

Sell them the solution.

Initially, you'll probably frame your solution as an eBook. They're free to make, free to deliver, and you can put them on ClickBank (*www.ClickBank.com*). ClickBank will handle the accounting, keep up with affiliate sales, send your affiliates their money, and send you your money every two weeks.

You may discover an olde Scottish tome that is in the public domain that is just chock full of golfing wisdom. Turn that sucker into a PDF, and sell it.

Remember, we're selling information. You can also package the information as an audio MP3, which you can also put on ClickBank.

Lately, I've been having a lot of fun with video. The Internet is just too slow to deliver professional video online. That will change. About half the country, and a lot of the rest of the world, is still using dial-up, which is way too slow for video. That will change, too, but we're in a hurry, so, you'll have to deliver DVDs. This introduces a level of complexity to your Portable Empire that you may want to avoid for now.

(*www.PatOBryan.com/blog.htm* - 07/08/06 Selling the Solution - Every Problem Is a Product)

Imagine that your niche is golf. That's a great niche, because it's got a lot of very interesting problems.

You could create an "Introduction to Golfing," and then an eBook on how to choose the right golf clubs. Follow that up with "27 Things to Ask Your Golf Pro." "Reports from the World's Best Golf Courses," would be my next choice – and would lead to a nice tax-deductible vacation.

Over time, you'll establish relationships with a large group of people who rely on you to provide solutions to their golfing problems – and pay you for those solutions.

Get the picture?

CHAPTER 2

HOW TO CREATE VALUABLE INFORMATION PRODUCTS AUTOMATICALLY

You hear it all the time, don't you? "I've got this great idea for an eBook; I just don't know how to write it." Or, "I've been working on my eBook for months, but I just can't seem to finish it."

I've talked to potential authors who have spent years struggling to write their first eBook!

What if I could show you how to write an interesting and valuable eBook instantly and effortlessly? Would you be interested?

One of my favorite images in American Literature is the young Tom Sawyer, who was commanded to whitewash a fence. It was a boring, tedious job, and he really didn't want to do it.

Knowing that if you want something other than the obvious to happen you have to do something other than the obvious, Tom pretended to have so much fun white-washing that fence that other boys literally begged him to let them do it.

I've taken Tom's approach to fence painting and applied it to writing eBooks.

CHAPTER 3

WHY WRITE AN EBOOK?

There are several good reasons to become an eBook author.

1. Money. Information is big business. You can create a product once and sell it thousands or millions of times. Every aspect of the process can be automated except the actual writing – and with the tricks I'm about to show you, even the writing will be easy and painless.

2. Build your list. Every Internet marketer knows that "the gold is in the list." I've added thousands of names to my mailing list by giving away an eBook in exchange for email addresses. Once a person opts in to your list, you have their permission to contact them and tell them about the products you have for sale.

3. Increase your visibility and credibility. You will be viewed as an authority on the subjects you write about, provided you write informative and accurate eBooks. If you can persuade a more prominent author to co-write with you, you increase your credibility.

In return, your co-author will receive the benefits of increased productivity, more visibility and more income.

4. *Drive traffic to your other projects.* Always include website addresses in the header of your eBooks. There are many opportunities to tempt your readers to explore your sales sites.

CHAPTER 4

WHAT TO WRITE ABOUT

I can remember a time when there was no such thing as an eBook. I suspect that in the future all books will be eBooks. Right now, the most successful eBooks are nonfiction.

A look at the best selling eBooks on ClickBank reveals titles like: "How to…," "The Ten Secrets of…," and "Get Paid to…"

There is a school of thought that says you should diligently research the search engines and current ClickBank inventory to find out what people want and then write your eBook targeting the identified market, regardless of your interest in or knowledge of the subject.

This strikes me as similar to trying to drive while looking in your rear view mirror. Although research is good, this particular research only tells you what's behind you. It seems to come from a mindset of scarcity – as if you can only write one eBook! With the tools I'm about to give you, you can write an eBook a day if you want to.

The "next big thing" is going to come from someone who comes up with something new and different – why shouldn't it be you?

You should pick a subject that interests you, and one that you already know something about. If you have experience working on cars, you might consider writing a book on basic automobile maintenance.

Target a specific market. This eBook is for people who are writing their first eBook. If I were writing for Literature Majors in Graduate School, I would write an entirely different book.

Using our example of a book on automobile maintenance, you could target housewives, teenage girls, senior citizens, or people who own vintage Fords. In my opinion, a book on that subject that would be valuable to all those groups would be too long and complex for the eBook format.

CHAPTER 5

THE PUBLIC DOMAIN

For information about copyrights and the public domain, go to *http://www.Copyright.gov/circs/circ1.html*

Here's a brief run-down of the rules. I am not a lawyer, and this is not meant to be legal advice. If you're unsure, hire a lawyer!

Almost anything copyrighted before 1923 is in the public domain.

Some works published between 1923 and 1989 without proper copyright notice, and works published before 1964 whose copyrights weren't renewed, may be in the public domain.

Tony Laidig's book, *The Public Domain Code Book* (*www.PublicDomain-CodeBook.com*), has an exhaustive list of resources for finding public domain books. I recommend it highly.

Several Internet marketing fortunes have been made by recycling out of print books that have lapsed into the public domain. The laws concerning public domain have changed through the years.

There is a virtually endless supply of valuable and useful books that, with a new title and a modern cover, still have lots of life – and sales – left in them.

Once you're absolutely sure that the book you're interested in recycling is in the public domain, you're free to copy, augment, edit, repackage and sell it. There are some tricks to this – if you're not sure, ask a lawyer – but once you've learned the ground rules, you've got the accumulated inventory of centuries of writing at your disposal.

If you use a public domain work as a starting place, and add your own original material to it, you have created a "derivative work" and may be able to copyright that!

Here's a hint: almost all government publications are in the public domain.

CHAPTER 6

FIND A WORK
IN THE PUBLIC DOMAIN

Aquick Google search found these resources. This will change daily.

Project Gutenberg, at *http://www.Gutenberg.net* has over ten thousand books online. Many of them are in the public domain. Their license page, *http://www.Gutenberg.net/license*, explains the rules. Project Gutenberg mainly focuses on literature.

Books for a Buck, at *http://www.BooksForABuck.com/general/pubsources.html*, has an index of sources for free books, many of them in the public domain.

The Alex Catalogue of Electronic Texts, *http://www.InfoMotions.com/alex2/*, has an online search engine for finding public domain works.

The Internet Public Library, *http://www.ipl.org/div/books/*, is another search engine for finding public domain works.

The Digital Library at Dartmouth, *http://www.Dartmouth.edu/~libcirc/eBooks.shtml*, has some good links.

CHAPTER 7
REBRAND A PUBLIC DOMAIN WORK

I f you find a book in the public domain, or acquire the rights to an existing book, you have the option of "rebranding" that book.

There have been several successful eBooks whose authors merely changed the title and cover on existing public domain works.

If a book is out of print but not in the public domain, there's a good chance the author will sell you all or part of the rights.

Once you've acquired your book, you need to "rebrand" it. A great title and cover is all you need.

There is an art to creating effective titles for eBooks. The title is your headline. An interesting and arresting title is your most effective selling tool.

Remember that people buy benefits. How those benefits are created is less interesting to a reader than what the benefits are. Remember, the question your potential buyer is asking is, "what's in it for me?"

A book on investing? The benefits would be increased financial security, increased buying power, and financial freedom. The title, "Fire Your Boss" will sell more eBooks than "A Comparative Analysis of Market Index Financial Products," although both books might have the same content.

Look for the positive outcome for your reader. Will your recipe book help them lose weight or find a mate? "Sexy Salads" will probably sell a lot more copies than "Roughage Recipes for a Clean Colon." A lot more.

CHAPTER REVIEW

REBRAND A PUBLIC DOMAIN BOOK

1. What sources can you find, online and offline, for public domain material?

2. From these sources, what material can you find that solves a common or interesting problem in an interesting way?

3. What steps can you take to make your public domain information relevant and interesting for a modern audience? Remember that sometimes all you need is a new title and cover.

CHAPTER 8

WRITE A WORKBOOK OR STUDY GUIDE USING A PUBLIC DOMAIN WORK

One of the fastest ways to create a new product using existing material is to write a workbook or study guide.

My first eBook, co-written with Dr. Joe Vitale, was *The Think and Grow Rich Workbook.* Thousands of people have found success by applying the techniques that Napoleon Hill describes in his book.

It was Joe who pointed out that one edition of the book had lapsed into the public domain. Only one edition, and I'm not going to tell you which one. Don't try this at home.

Sitting in my favorite coffee shop, I harvested the rich fruit from the book and reverse engineered it. I sent it to Joe and he added his hypnotic contributions. Voila! An eBook was born.

We gave away a copy to everybody who subscribed to the Milagro Research Institute ezine, Milagro World (*www.MilagroWorld.com*). This increased our list by several thousand names in a very short time, and has resulted in some exciting viral marketing.

Since we launched that workbook, I've learned a valuable lesson. Although a book may be out of print, its title may be a "trademark." I learned this lesson from the Napoleon Hill Foundations very efficient legal department. It turns out that, although the book and the title have lapsed into the public domain, the title "Think and Grow Rich," is a trademark of the Napoleon Hill Foundation.

They also claim that the words "Grow Rich," when used in the title of a product will create confusion in the consumer's mind.

You can research trademarks at *http://www.Uspto.gov/.*

The concept of "confusion in the consumer's mind" is pretty vague – and I suspect the party with the most predatory attorneys will prevail if it ever came to litigation. The mere threat of litigation is enough to cause most authors, including me, to rename their products.

When I write, I like to work from an outline. Many authors do. It's a great tool for organizing your thoughts. You can break a large, intimidating project down into smaller, more manageable projects.

To create a workbook, it's useful to work backwards and make an outline from the existing book. Write down the title of the chapter. Now go through the chapter and write down the major points. The idea is to strip away everything but the essential facts.

Once you've distilled the chapter down to the bare necessities, put it back together again in your own words. Pretend that you're using your notes to tell a friend what the chapter is about. If your friends are anything like mine, you'll want to tell them in clear simple sentences.

You can increase the value of your workbook, and get more mileage out of your work, by including a chapter quiz. Go back and pick out a handful of the most important facts from each chapter and restate them in question form.

For example, if one of your facts is "The capital of Texas is Austin," you might write "What is the Capital of Texas?" I told you this was easy!

CHAPTER REVIEW

WRITE A WORKBOOK OR STUDY GUIDE USING A PUBLIC DOMAIN WORK

1. What online resources can you find to help you identify and obtain a public domain book?

2. What public domain book do you think would make an interesting workbook?

3. Outline the book – write down the chapter heading, and list the major points from each chapter.

4. Rewrite each chapter using the material from your outline. Remember to write in a conversational style.

5. Make a chapter review – what are the most important points from the chapter?

6. Remember to include links to your other projects!

CHAPTER 9

GET OTHERS TO WRITE YOUR EBOOK

Another strategy for producing an eBook is to ask others to write it for you. Some of the most successful eBook promotions have featured eBooks with multiple authors.

Why would an author give you a chapter for your book?

Because you will encourage them to include their contact information and links to their web pages, that's why. The more copies of your book that you sell or give away, the more traffic they get to their sales sites. More traffic equals more sales.

Here's how I have used this technique.

At one of our weekly mastermind meetings, I cracked a joke about the myth of making a passive income (*www.MythOfPassiveIncome.com*). I was whining because I had spent two whole hours filling orders and answering customer service emails.

This was the Internet age – I was supposed to be sitting on the beach smoking a Cuban cigar and drinking espresso while the money magically appeared in my bank account, wasn't I?

The reality, as most successful Internet marketers will tell you if you catch them out of the public eye, is that most successful Internet marketers work long hours to create passive income. Especially in the beginning of your Internet marketing career, passive income is a myth.

Dr. Joe Vitale laughed at my joke, and then decided it would make an interesting book. So he contacted several of the top Internet marketers and asked them to write a chapter about their passive income experiences. In a couple of weeks, we had over twenty chapters, from some of the biggest names in the business.

You can see the final product at *www.MythOfPassiveIncome.com*.

This technique will work for almost any subject. For example, if you wanted to write a book about running a successful ezine, you could email the authors of the most successful ezines and ask them to contribute a chapter.

I suspect most of them would jump at the chance. Every copy of your eBook will be an advertisement for their ezine.

When it came time to approach joint-venture partners for the eBook, we approached the co-authors. They were happy to make money from the eBook. Of course, it would be interesting to their lists – since they're in it.

This generated a lot of sales, but more importantly, each person they sent to our site had the opportunity to sign up for our list. This is a great technique for "creaming" another marketer's list. We were able to identify, and gain access to, the members of their list that were interested in our products.

This has led to some great relationships with our new subscribers, and subsequent sales of other products.

Get the idea?

CHAPTER REVIEW

GET OTHERS TO WRITE YOUR EBOOK FOR YOU

1. What problems can you think of that could be solved by experts?

2. Who are these experts?

3. Contact Them – Find their email addresses, write their publishers, join their lists, and be creative! Don't get discouraged if they don't all respond. Remember to be courteous and respectful – they're doing you a favor.

4. How do you want to format your book? You can have a chapter from each expert, or format your book into a conversation, or record and edit it onto a CD. Be creative!

5. If at all possible, write a chapter for your book yourself. One of your goals is to have your name linked with known experts as often as possible – that's how you become a known expert!

CHAPTER 10

USE INTERVIEWS TO WRITE AN EBOOK

A variation on having others write your book for you is to use interviews.

This is just a little more work, but there are a lot of benefits to this method. Remember that the interview can be conducted by phone, in person, by email – sometimes, the method you use to interview the expert can be a selling point. Be creative!

People who might not take the time to write a chapter are more likely to have a conversation with you, especially if you entice them with an ethical bribe – in this case, you can offer to include their contact and sales information in the chapter you create from the interview.

Remember, these interviews can be done over the phone or through email.

For example, suppose you wanted to write an eBook about the best way to buy a used car. You could arrange to talk with a broad range of used car salesmen. What are their tricks? What techniques do they use to get customers to buy? What should a customer ask? What should a customer be afraid of or concerned about?

31

Most salesmen will happily talk about their business, if you can convince them that it will attract more customers.

In this case, I'd ask them about the dirty tricks other salesmen use.

If you're writing an eBook about a topic you're very familiar with, you can interview yourself!

Once you've got your interviews, you've converted your authoring problem to a typing problem. You can even hire a transcription service to type it for you.

Writing your book from interviews has a hidden benefit – you now have an audio product to sell! You can use your interview tapes as the source material to create CDs or you can convert them to MP3's and sell them as digital products.

One example of an interview MP3 product is at *www.e-BookProblemSolver.com.* I interviewed Dr. Joe Vitale on the subject of eBook production and marketing, converted the interview into MP3's and put them online. After listening to that interview, you should be able to come up with a topic, write the eBook, get it online, and sell it. The whole production took less than four hours to create – and was a lot of fun.

Right now, the most popular eBooks are the ones that explain how to do something: how to save money, how to make a web page, how to fix a car, how to satisfy your lover, how to bake a great cheesecake – even how to write an eBook!

You're looking for an expert, but don't get in a rut about what constitutes an "expert." Here are some potential subjects for your interview. I'll bet you can think of many more.

Real Estate Agent – Real estate is the most expensive purchase most of us will make. People want information about how to make these purchases intelligently.

- How to Finance Your First Real Estate Purchase
- How to Rent to Own
- How to Sell Your House Yourself without an Agent
- How to Prepare Your House to Get the Best Price When You Sell It – here's a hint – bake bread before the prospective buyer shows up!
- How to Qualify for a Mortgage
- How to Get the Most House for Your Money
- How to Make Money on Rental Property

Insurance Agent – Insurance is a subject that is mystifying and scary to most people.

- How to Buy Life Insurance
- How to Buy Health Insurance
- Different Types of Life Insurance – Who Should Buy What?
- Major Medical versus Full Coverage

Day Care Center worker/owner –

- How to Find a Safe Day Care Center
- What are the Dangers?
- Licensing of Day Care Centers
- Montessori versus Traditional

There is no limit to this – find a problem and solve it. Then sell the solution.

Coffee Shop Employee –

- How to Make the Perfect Cup of Coffee
- The Best Beans

- **Easy Mistakes Everybody Makes**
- **Eco-Friendly Coffee – Why It's Good for You and Good for the Planet**
- **Grumpy Customers – Nightmare Stories from the Coffee Shop**

Internet Gurus – This is an area that is saturated. If you're going to write about making money online, you need to have a unique perspective. One of the most popular eBooks right now is a series of interviews with "unknown" online marketers. Find an angle that nobody else has exploited.

Here are a few I've come up with:

Secret Lives - What's unusual and unknown about Internet marketing celebrities? Do they play guitar, paint pictures, climb mountains, write children's books, or work for charity? People are interested in the human side of celebrities.

Rags to Riches – This one always works.

Unusual Success – Everybody markets information products. Can you find someone who markets something really unusual online?

Riches to Rags – Mistakes are how we learn. It's less painful to learn from someone else's mistakes.

High School Students – This is a big market. When you add in their parents, it's one of the biggest.

- **How to Make Great Grades**
- **How to Use High School to Prepare for College**

- **Social Games and How to Win Them**
- **How to Be Yourself and Survive High School**
- **Fashion Secrets for High School Students**

College Students –

How to Make Money While You're in College – See if you can get Michael Dell!

How to Start Your Career While You're Still in College. Many industries, including banking, financial planning, sales, and CPA's have mentor programs for students studying their field.

- **How to Survive College**
- **99 Ways to Pay for College**
- **How to Get a Grant, Scholarship or Loan for College**

Retirees –

Just because someone has reached the mandatory retirement age in their industry doesn't mean they immediately lose their value, and because they are retired, they probably will welcome the opportunity to help you with your book!

Industry survey – What jobs provided the most satisfaction?

- **How to Retire with a Comfortable Income**
- **How to Survive Retirement**
- **Insider Secrets to… (whatever industry they retired from)**

I hope you're getting the idea that almost anybody can be an expert and a resource for a profitable eBook if you create the right questions.

CHAPTER REVIEW

USING INTERVIEWS TO
WRITE AN EBOOK

1. What is an interesting problem that could be solved by talking to an expert?

2. Who is this expert? Find him/her.

3. Come up with the questions. Find the problem. Lead the expert to tell you his/her solution.

4. What method will you use to record the interview? Email, phone, or personal conversation?

5. Write it down. Sell it.

CHAPTER 11

USE SEARCH ENGINES TO WRITE YOUR EBOOK

Another eBook-generating idea is actually as old as graduate school, but the Internet makes it practical. It's called "research."

The word "research" brings back memories of confusion and frustration for me. Have they found the sadist that came up with the Dewey decimal system and strung him up yet? I never did understand it.

Google, on the other hand, I understand. Without having to resort to card files or surly librarians, I can type in the subject of my prospective eBook and hit "enter." This will return pages and pages of links to information on my topic.

For example, lately I've been working on *Meditate for Success.* It's an eBook about how you can use a combination of modern technology and ancient mind control methods as your secret weapon to get ahead of your competition. As a happy coincidence, I produce audio products that use modern technology and ancient mind control methods. You can find out all about them at *http://www.MilagroResearchInstitute.com/mmm01.htm* and *http://www.InstantChange.com.*

That one sentence was about all I could think of to say about it, which would have made for a short and disappointing eBook. So I zipped over to Google and typed in "benefits of meditation."

Wow. Over eight thousand websites just brimming with information, case studies, galvanic skin response test results, brain wave scans, and magazine articles appeared out of hyperspace.

I grabbed the most interesting and compelling benefits and pasted them into my eBook. Under each benefit, I wrote a short paragraph describing the benefit and how it was achieved. Then I erased the stuff I had pasted, leaving my original work – a completed chapter on the benefits of meditation.

Using this technique, I believe I could write a believable eBook on almost any subject, and so could you.

CHAPTER REVIEW

USING SEARCH ENGINES TO WRITE YOUR EBOOK

1. Describe your problem in question form. For example, if the problem you want to write about is fear of public speaking, you might frame your question as "How do you overcome fear of public speaking?" I Just entered that question into Google and got 426,000 web pages to use as resources!

2. What are your questions? Find the solution to your problem.

3. Copy and paste the most interesting and relevant information into your document.

4. Under each fact, write a paragraph expanding and explaining it.

5. Erase your original "copy and paste" research.

CHAPTER 12

USE LISTS TO WRITE YOUR EBOOK

Another popular eBook format is the "list." If you can think of 10, 21, 101 things that go together, you've got an eBook.

For example, my friend, Nerissa Oden, wrote an eBook called "101 Fun Things You Can Do with Your New Digital Camera."

List books are easy to write.

Here are a few ideas I came up with over a cup of coffee:

25 Tricks for Saving Money on Gasoline

101 eBook Ideas

10 Steps to the Perfect Cup of Coffee

17 Things You Must Know about Wine

99 Great Sandwich Ideas

19 Things to Look for When You're Looking for a Computer

111 Dating Tips for the Shy Man

1001 Ways to Make Money with Your Laptop Computer

12 Secrets of Automobile Maintenance

25 Things Your Banker Will NOT Tell You

CHAPTER REVIEW

USING LISTS TO WRITE YOUR EBOOK

1. What problem are you going to solve with this eBook?

2. How many solutions can you come up with? List them.

3. Get some coffee

CHAPTER 13

WHAT _____ CAN TEACH US
ABOUT _____

This chapter started as an article called "What Tom Sawyer Taught Me About Writing eBooks."

My friend, Bill Hibbler, wrote a popular series of articles called "What American Idol Can Teach Us about Marketing" that you can read at *http://www.eCommerceConfidential.com/articles.html*.

The more arresting your source, the more interest there will be in your book. Look for interesting juxtapositions and surprising contrasts.

Here are a few ideas:

What Sex Workers Can Teach Us about Politics

What Thomas Jefferson Can Teach Us about Love

What Captain Kangaroo Taught Me about Physics

What Jesse James Can Teach Us about Banking

William Shakespeare on Marketing

Gertrude Stein's Secrets of Communication

What Madonna Can Show Us about Marketing

CHAPTER REVIEW

WHAT _____ CAN
TEACH US ABOUT _____

1. What is your target problem?

2. Who are the most outrageous and interesting cultural figures you can think of who could shed some light on your target problem?

3. What would your expert have to say on the subject?

4. Be creative. This is an area where humor is your friend.

CHAPTER 14

NOW WHAT?

E asy, isn't it?

How many eBooks have you written so far?

Keep at it. Use every new eBook as an opportunity to promote your previous eBooks.

Now that you're an eBook author, you're going to be interested in how to market your eBook.

CHAPTER 15

THE ABSOLUTE BEGINNER'S GUIDE TO COPYWRITING

basic knowledge of psychology is useful when you're writing sales copy. If you're curious about why people do what people do, go grab Influence 101. It's at *http://www.Influence101.com*

CHAPTER 16

THE BASICS

What's the big secret that copywriters use to write effective copy?

Here it is: Everybody is in a trance. The number of people who are self-actualized and completely aware is so small that you can discount them when you're writing sales copy. The people who are going to read your sales copy are caught up in their lives.

You might want to check out the movie, *What the Bleep Do We Know?* It's the most useful explanation of this phenomenon I've ever seen.

People are living inside their heads.

They just drove home from a job they hate to a spouse who doesn't understand them, or understands them far too well. Their bratty kids are whining about some silly thing. The bills are due, and they don't have the money to pay. Their mind is anywhere but where they are.

Or...

They've spent the entire day changing diapers, mopping floors, and watching daytime T.V. Their mind is on the cross-dressing librarian they couldn't tear themselves away from on the box, their feet hurt, and they're worried sick about some movie star's love life.

Or...

The limo driver was late, the board meeting was hell, and Warren Buffet just dumped his holdings in their publicly traded corporation, and is advising the world to do the same. The S.E.C. is skeptical about last year's financials, and the little weasel in accounting who threatened to squeal hasn't been at work in three days.

Your mission, should you accept it, is to know exactly who you're writing to, and walk a few thousand miles in their shoes. Get inside their mind. Find the pain, and then frame your solution to soothe their pain.

I've seen grown men cry as they sat at their desk, visualizing their readers, and their reader's lives.

That's the big secret.

Now, let's look at the nuts and bolts of copywriting.

We're going to focus on the "big seven" components of a well-written sales page.

1. **Headline**
2. **Bullet-points**
3. **Subheads**
4. **The Body**
5. **The Guarantee**
6. **The Close**
7. **The P.S.**

Once you master those, you're ready to start writing copy.

CHAPTER 17

THE HEADLINE

Ninety percent of your effort should go into writing your headline, because 90% of the effectiveness of your copy depends on it.

Write a lot of headlines. Fifty isn't too many.

The purpose of the headline is to pull the reader's mind out of its daily trance and into your sales copy.

Professional copywriters, who are an educated, savvy bunch, read the magazines you find at the check-out counter at the grocery store like textbooks. "Elvis Marries 2-Headed Space Alien in Shotgun Ceremony!" "World Ending Thursday, 7:13 P.M., According to Secret Prediction!" "Oprah Loses 250 Pounds Eating Ice Cream – You Can, Too!"

That sort of thing.

Why? Because they stop you in your tracks and make you want to know more. Intellectually, you know they're bull-poop, but people don't buy with their intellect, they buy with their emotions.

There are an infinite number of ways to approach the writing of headlines, but let's confine ourselves to five good ones for now.

CHAPTER 18

THE QUESTION

Ask a question that can't immediately be answered with "yes" or "no."

"Do You Make These Seven Copywriting Mistakes?"

You can't answer that unless you know what they are. You have to read the first sentence of the copy to find out. You want to know, don't you? What are those mistakes? Do you make them? What are you going to do about it?

Let's try another one.

"How Can YOU Fire Your Boss?"

Again, you won't know if you don't read the first sentence of the copy.

"What If You Could Double Your Sales In Ten Days?"

You can turn simple sentences into questions:

"You Want Financial Security, Don't You?"

"She Deserves the Best, Doesn't She?"

Here's a special kind of question headline:

"What Can a 29 Year Old Bottle Washer From Cleveland, Texas Teach You about the 17 Shameful Secrets Of Shampoo?"

How can you resist?

CHAPTER 19

THE CALL-OUT

This is the easiest headline you can write, and it's very effective if your product is for a specific niche.

If you're selling a headache remedy, try "Headache Sufferers!"

If you're selling guitar strings, try "Guitar Players!"

If you're selling investments, try "Investors!"

You'll only get the attention of the very narrow group that you "call out," but if your product is that tightly focused, that's all you need.

CHAPTER 20

A LITTLE PSYCHOLOGY

One of the psychological tools I discuss in Influence101 is "Social Proof." You can get your copy of this audio home-study course at *http://www.Influence101.com*.

Humans are herd animals. If "everybody" is doing something, then "you" must need to do it, too. Everybody else can't be wrong, can they?

History is full of examples of "everybody" being wrong. "Social Proof" is how peer group pressure works.

The fashion industry, the soft drink industry, the religion industry, and the politics industry know this one, and use it all the time.

We can use this principle to craft effective headlines.

One that has been over-used lately, but is a good example is:

"Who Else Wants to Make $20,000 a Week?"

Another way to use it is:

"Don't Get Left Behind!"

Or, "20,000 Blind Albino Aviators Can't Be Wrong!"

Intellectually, you know that they can. Writing sales copy has nothing to do with the intellect. People buy with their emotions and justify it with their intellect.

CHAPTER 21

IMAGINE THAT...

Create a picture that draws your reader in.

"Imagine How Much Freedom You'll Have When You Master Copywriting!"

"Picture This – Your First Million Dollars!"

The trick here is to paint a vague picture that is enticing, and let the reader fill in the details.

In the headline, "Picture Yourself in the Car of Your Dreams!" the reader will do exactly that – providing the make, model, year and color for you.

The more detail you provide, the tighter your focus – and the smaller your potential target.

CHAPTER 22

QUOTES

nything with quotation marks around it will stand out. "The Best Cigar I Ever Smoked," Britney Spears.

"All My Men Wear Levi's," Elton John

"They Laughed When I Sat Down at the Piano, but When I Began to Play…" This may be the most famous headline in history, by the way. It ran, successfully, for decades.

CHAPTER 23

STEAL THIS AD

As you start thinking like a copywriter, you'll start noticing advertisements from a different perspective. Pay special attention to the headlines that get used over and over. Major advertisers are constantly testing headlines – if you notice an ad that runs for several months with the same headline, write that headline down!

It's working.

Another interesting thing to note about successful copywriters: they steal. Every copywriter worth his salt has something called a "swipe file." This is where they put copies of ads that they like. When it's time for them to write a headline, the first thing they do is go to their swipe file and try to find one they can modify to fit their assignment.

Advertising may not be the oldest profession – although, it's closely related. It has, however, been around a long, long, long time. Occasionally, some genius will come up with a headline that hasn't been used before, but it's very rare. Trust me, start snagging great ads, and start your own swipe file.

Caveat – don't steal word-for-word. Use your swipe file for inspiration.

As you read the ad, see if you can analyze it to discover why it worked,

69

and use that knowledge to create one that will work the same way.

Another interesting thing about copywriters – they sue. For example, there have been instances where a copywriter has been so impressed by Ted Nicholas' copy that he used it verbatim. He regretted it almost instantly.

CHAPTER 24

BULLET POINTS

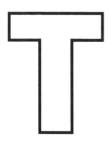here are at least three kinds of readers:

1. **Those who will read every word you write.**
2. **Those who skim, focusing on headlines, bullet points, and major points.**
3. **Those who read the headline and then skip to the offer.**

They all read the P.S., by the way.

As you design your copy, you need to keep all three readers in mind. You need to tell your story with your headline, sub-headlines, bullet points, and P.S., for the benefit of the skimmers – and you need to do it in a way that allows your copy to flow smoothly.

Bullet points are used to call attention to benefits.

Do you know the difference between a feature and a benefit? It's a little tricky, but it's a distinction you need to learn.

"Fine German engineering allows this car to cruise at 120 MPH!" is a feature.

"You can be playing golf while the others are still driving!" is a benefit.

Here's another example:

"This vacuum cleaner has suction pressure in excess of 9,000 PSI.!" is a feature.

"This vacuum cleaner will get your carpet so clean your neighbors will turn green with envy!" is a benefit.

Actually, "your neighbors will turn green with envy" is a benefit of the benefit "will get your carpets so clean."

Are you starting to see the difference? The feature is the description. The benefit is what it does for you.

Let's look at another one.

"This pizza contains broccoli, spinach, and spirulina," discusses features.

"Healthy pizza for building strong, sexy bodies," discusses benefits.

Now let's look for a benefit of the benefit:

"Healthy pizza that will make you so strong that girls will be asking you out!" The benefit of the benefit "so strong" is "girls will be asking you out."

One of the most famous copywriting stories comes from David Ogilvy. He had to write a sales page for a luxury car. Writing good sales copy requires intense research. He interviewed engineers and sales staff. He examined the car.

Finally, he read the technical reports. Over a hundred pages into a dry, boring technical report he came across the sentence, "At 60 miles per hour, the loudest sound you'll hear is the ticking of the clock."

He used that as his headline. Notice, he didn't say a word about the engineering excellence of the car, or the seals around the windows. Those are features. He found the hidden benefit.

Bullet points are only slightly less important than headlines. Almost all of your readers will read them. If you need ten bullet points, write a hundred, and then choose the best ten.

CHAPTER 25

SUB-HEADS

Sub-headlines are like bullet points, but they stand alone and introduce a new section of copy.

Everything we've discussed about headlines and bullet points applies to sub-headlines.

Use them to grab your reader by the shirt collar and make him or her read the following copy.

Here are some examples of sub-headlines:

"But Wait – There's More!" Personal note: whenever I hang out with copywriters, I'm silently watching the second hand on my watch. It's only a matter of time before one of them quotes this sub-headline, and then the others laugh uncontrollably.

"New For 2006!" would be a way to introduce benefits and features that have been changed for the new product year.

"How can a 165 year old technology revolutionize your sales path?" is a sub-head that was used for our very successful "Think and Grow Rich Automatically" sales page. Please note that we have changed the title. See Chapter One.

"Living a Lifestyle beyond the Dreams of Avarice" helped us sell a pile of "The Myth of Passive Income." (*www.MythOfPassiveIncome.com*)

Get the idea? A sub-headline is just like any other headline, except it leads into a specific section of copy. When you're writing your list of potential headlines, be sure and note the ones that would make good sub-heads.

CHAPTER 26

THE BODY

This is the meat and potatoes of sales copy.

This is where you identify your customer's pain, and provide him with the magic secret that will make the pain go away.

You may be wondering, "How long should the copy be?" The answer is, as long as it needs to be. There is a rule of thumb that states that the more expensive the item you're trying to sell, the longer the copy needs to be.

Don't be afraid of long copy. Remember your three kinds of readers. A person who is contemplating a purchase, especially the purchase of an expensive item, wants to know all there is to know about the item.

The very first step is to visualize who you're writing to. What trance are they in as they begin to read?

What did they do all day? Was it fun? What do they want to do? Are they hungry? Are they thirsty? Are they broke? Are they looking for the perfect diamond ring?

You've used your headline to stop them in their tracks.

You've listed a few bullet points to make them curious.

You've got their attention with your sub-head.

Now you've got to lead them to the bottom of the page and help them press the "buy now" button.

Try to meet them where they are and take them with you. Imagine their objections and address them in your copy.

Avoid using big words when smaller words will do, and adjust your vocabulary to fit your reader. If you're advertising reverse amortization mortgages in the secondary market, you're going to use a completely different vocabulary than you will when you're selling diapers.

One way to pull them into your copy is to tell them a story.

I've used this one several times: "I used to be a broke blues guitar player, living on $30-$50 a night, a few nights a week. I lived in a mobile home, until it got repossessed. I know more ways to cook pinto beans than anybody else in North America, because pinto beans are about all we could afford to buy at the grocery store."

Hopefully, by this point in the story, I've got my reader nodding his head. He's been broke before. He's identifying with my story, and putting himself in my place.

He's ready for some good news:

"Then, one day I met Dr. Joe Vitale at a restaurant in Wimberley, Texas, and he handed me that book. What book? Spiritual Marketing. The secrets contained in that book gave me the knowledge and power to reframe my life, and create a lifestyle that gives me freedom, happiness and pleasure."

If I've done my job, my reader is asking, "Where can I get that book?"

Your story doesn't have to be about you. It does have to draw the reader into your sales copy. Use your story as an opportunity to stress the benefits of the product in a personal way.

Another strategy for writing compelling sales copy is to round up your best sub-headlines and put them in a logical order. Then use your copy to expand and explain the benefits mentioned in the sub-head.

Let's look at some other strategies for leading our customer to the "buy now" button.

One technique I rely on a lot is the "problem-solution" copy.

You might start out by asking a question:

"Do You Have Dandruff?" for example.

Then describe the heartbreak of dandruff. Maybe tell a story about a man who lost his wife, his job, and his self-respect because of dandruff.

That's the problem.

Then, just before our poor dandruff sufferer hangs himself from a shower rod, you present the solution.

"Rub this duck oil on your head twice a day, and you won't have to worry about losing your wife, your job, or your self-respect."

I'm exaggerating just a little – the gym where I work out has a TV, and today I went during the day while the soap operas were on. Daytime TV is pretty educational if you're a student of advertising.

I'm not exaggerating very much. For certain audiences, that approach works like a charm.

With appropriate modification, it will work for any audience.

CHAPTER 27

TESTIMONIALS

The sales copy can contain testimonials, or you can use them to break up the copy into sections.

Testimonials are essential. Instead of just one person (you) who has a financial interest in the sale telling them how great the product is, you can gather a crowd to tell them.

The two best kinds of testimonials are from experts and people just like your customer.

There is a trick to getting a testimonial, even from an expert, by the way.

It's a secret, but I'll tell you.

"You ask."

Don't tell anybody.

Use testimonials to build the case for your product.

CHAPTER 28

THE GUARANTEE

Use your guarantee to shift the risk from the purchaser to you.

You want your customer to feel totally confident when they buy your product. If they feel like they're going to be stuck with it if they don't like it, they won't buy it. This is especially true on the Internet, where they can't touch, or even see the actual product.

Here's a rule of thumb I learned from a very famous copywriter who was speaking at a seminar – "The longer the guarantee, the lower the return rate."

Think about it. If you know you've got three days to decide if you like something, you're going to be in a pretty big hurry to find something you don't like. If you know you've got a year, or a lifetime, you don't feel any urgency. In fact, you may forget about it completely.

I believe in strong guarantees.

I watched Dr. Joe Vitale offer a "double your money back" guarantee on a product that sold for almost a thousand dollars. That's a very gutsy guarantee. It worked. He sold almost half a million dollars worth of product in just a few days – and one of the reasons was that outrageous guarantee.

ClickBank, and most merchant account companies, keep a reserve to pay for refunds. They use an algorithm based on your refund history, the price of the product, and the phase of the moon – I guess. I really don't know how they do it, but I do know that they keep part of the sales revenue for a long time to make sure there's money there to pay for refunds.

It's worth it.

CHAPTER 29

THE CLOSE

This is where you ask for the sale.

There's no point being shy now. Either you've built a strong emotional case for your product or you haven't.

Ask them to click the "buy now" button.

The trend right now in online sales is to hit them high, and then offer a lower price.

Like this:

"What would you pay for that kind of freedom? What's your financial independence worth to you?

You're probably thinking, "At least a million dollars."

And you're right – but because you're one of my treasured subscribers, I'm offering it for only $497...but wait, there's more!

If you buy today, or anytime before next Tuesday, you can have our Guide to Financial Freedom for only $17 – but hurry, this is a limited time offer!"

Again, I exaggerated for effect – but all the pieces are there. Establish a high value for your product, and then give a believable reason why it's cheaper in your offer. Create a sense of urgency – and stick to it. If you say that the price is going up on Tuesday, make darn sure you raise the price on Tuesday.

The close is where you mention the bonuses.

Whenever another author asks me if I've got anything laying around they can use for a bonus, I always answer "yes," even if I have to write it specifically for their project. Most marketers and authors are the same way.

Why?

Because we embed links to our web pages and our products in those bonuses. They are an excellent tool for driving traffic to our websites. The more traffic, the more sales for us.

You will have no trouble gathering up as many bonuses as you need.

Let's say you round up ten eBooks as bonuses, and can realistically valuate them at $30 each. That's $300 in bonuses that you can give away that didn't cost you a cent.

Those bonuses will make your "close" a whole lot easier to write.

Like this:

Buy "Grow Tomatoes Automatically" for only $17, and get these bonuses, valued at $300, absolutely free!

Remember, people buy with their emotions and justify the purchase with their intellect. What sort of emotional response do you think you're going to get when you offer to trade $317 worth of product for $17 in currency?

Bonuses make sales.

CHAPTER 30

THE P.S.

After you've asked for the sale, you sign the sales copy and go home, right?

Wrong.

One of the most important lines on your sales page is your P.S. Put it right under your signature.

Everybody reads the P.S.

This is where you restate the most important aspect of your sales letter. Like this:

P.S. There is no risk on your part – our products are guaranteed for your lifetime, and the lifetime of anybody who looks like you. Buy now!

Or –

P.S. Don't wait – offer ends tomorrow!

Use the P.S. to convince the reader who has passed right by the "buy now" button to retrace his steps and buy.

Some copywriters will add a P.P.S. and a P.P.P.S.

I don't know if there is an upper limit to the number of these things that can be used effectively. I try to limit myself to two.

CHAPTER 31

WHAT TO DO NEXT

A lthough we've only been together a short time, you now know more about copywriting than 90% of the people who are attempting to market their products on the Internet.

You certainly know more than I knew when I wrote my first sales page!

In the relatively short time I've been in the "Internet Marketing" business, I've had a lot of help. I couldn't have accomplished what I have without it. Would you like some help?

Recently, I've started promoting the "Your Portable Empire" (*www.YourPortableEmpire.com*) un-seminar. The first one was in Austin, in May, 2006. The second was September 22-24, 2006. It's an on-going series.

The un-seminar is a completely new format – there is a lot of pre-seminar training, which ensures that the attendees show up with rough drafts of their sales letter, their product, and their email marketing plans.

The un-seminar is focused on exactly and only what you need and the speakers are the acknowledged experts in their field.

At the un-seminar, the speakers do intense, one-on-one training. The attendees leave with a completely functioning business. It's an amazing opportunity to jump start your business and grab your freedom.

Of course, because each attendee gets so much personal attention from the speakers, we have to limit the seating. You can find out about availability at *http://www.PortableEmpire.com*.

The featured speaker on copywriting at these seminars is Dr. Joe Vitale.

If you're interested in really learning copywriting, go to *http://www. MrFire.com*, and talk to Joe.

CHAPTER 32

THE ABSOLUTE BEGINNER'S GUIDE TO JOINT VENTURE PROPOSALS

hat is a joint venture?

In Internet marketing terms, a joint venture is where a product owner and a list owner agree to work together for their mutual benefit.

My clients are all product developers, and so am I, so this will be written from that point of view.

CHAPTER 33

WHY JOINT VENTURE?

"Joint venture" is the answer to the question, "I've finished my eBook; what do I do now?"

You need to create a relationship with someone who has a list of people that they can offer your product to. More specifically, you're looking for people who already market products like yours to their list. It needs to be a good "fit."

The question you need to answer is "What's in it for me?" That's the question that will be on the top of your potential JV partner's mind. They want to make the most money with the least effort possible.

One day, you'll have your own huge list – until then, your job is to make it very, very easy for your JV partners.

Don't waste your time blindly sending JV proposals to absolute strangers. This almost never works.

Take the time to develop relationships with your potential JV partners. Subscribe to their ezines and newsletters. Research their businesses. Get to know them.

CHAPTER 34

LISTS

You'll hear it over and over again: "The gold is in your list."

When you're first starting out, you won't have a list. Every move you make should include building your list as one of your goals.

You will need to JV with people who have large lists. Some of the people on those lists will soon be on your list. That is the single most important factor in a JV agreement. You can market to these people for the rest of their lives.

Be prepared to give up a large chunk of your initial sales income to the list owner. The first sale is just that, the first sale. After you've acquired these customers, you can sell them other products and keep 100% of the money.

The gold is in your list. All other financial considerations are secondary.

Build your list.

When you're researching potential JV partners, you'll want to find out all you can about their lists.

This list needs to be "double opt-in," which means that subscribers have agreed to be on it, and then confirmed that agreement.

Single opt-in lists are not as responsive — I tend to avoid them.

People who market to "non-opt-in" lists are known as spammers.

There are two things to look at, initially, when analyzing a list: size and focus.

Size, in this instance, does matter. Bigger, in this case, is better. You're going to sell to a certain percentage of the people on the list. That percentage is a function of the "fit" or focus of the list and the effectiveness of your sales material. The more people on the list, the more sales that percentage represents.

The focus of the list is very important. If you've got a copywriting eBook, and you market it to a list of automobile mechanics, you're wasting your time.

Carefully research your potential JV partners to ensure that their list is a good "fit" for your product.

CHAPTER 35

WHO IS YOUR CUSTOMER?

The first step in creating a successful joint venture is to have a clear mental image of your potential customer.

Analyze your product, and then visualize who would benefit from it.

Some parameters to think about are:

1. What is your potential customer's level of expertise? Is he an "absolute beginner?" Is she an expert?

2. Where does your customer get their information? Some people only receive information from their television sets. Others read books. Others only get information from the Internet. Most people use a combination of sources, but you will notice trends. Laundry detergent is most effectively marketed on television. E-products, like eBooks, teleseminars, et cetera, are most effectively marketed on the Internet.

3. After you've identified the broad area where your customer gets his/her information, see how finely you can focus. Some

people only trust news from the *New York Times*. Others only trust Fox News. The same trend is true in Internet marketing. Some people are very tech oriented, and like a "nuts and bolts" proposal. Others respond to personality marketing, and are more interested in the seller than the product.

Get inside your customer's head and try to imagine what they are reading and listening to.

4. What vocabulary does your customer respond to? If you're selling pop-music ring tones for cell phones, your customers will expect a hip, young voice and vocabulary. If you're selling an eBook of stock market tips, a more mature tone is needed, along with a vocabulary that addresses the specific terminology of that market.

You're looking for a list that speaks to your customer.

CHAPTER 36

TYPES OF JOINT VENTURE PARTNERS

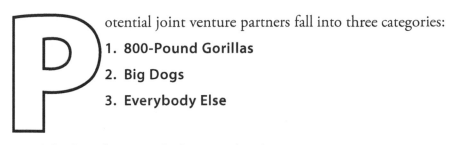

P otential joint venture partners fall into three categories:

1. **800-Pound Gorillas**
2. **Big Dogs**
3. **Everybody Else**

Let's look at them in a little more detail –

CHAPTER 37
STALKING THE 800-POUND GORILLA

The 800-pound gorillas are the household names. The Elvis's of Internet Marketing. You know who they are.

If you don't know who they are, go to *www.GuruDaq. com* and start reading. That site lists the most popular Internet marketing gurus in a faux stock market list. The ranking is irrelevant, but the same players show up on it in varying order every day. You can research these gorillas easily with the links on this page.

You want to create JV's with the gorillas before you contact the big dogs and affiliates. The 800-pound gorillas like drinking from a clear stream. If they have to compete with hundreds of small affiliates, they will probably pass on your proposal.

Ultimately, you want to establish relationships with the list owners who market to your customers.

Here are some strategies for establishing those relationships:

1) You know them (try giving them guitar lessons!)

2) You get to know them (meet them at a seminar),

3) **Work your way up through their organization – they've probably got a staff of people who go through JV proposals – they may get 20 to 50 a day, or**

4) **You get lucky – for example, your girlfriend's brother is listed on GuruDaq.**

You should immediately start sending proposals to the 800-pound gorillas who might be interested in marketing your product. We'll discuss how to create this proposal later in the book. This may be a long-term goal for you, but stick with it. Some of these guys can send a million emails with the wave of a wand.

Research these gurus, and identify the ones who are selling to the customers you want to sell to.

The next step is to find out where this customer goes online. Who is already talking to your customer? Who is already selling products to your customer?

Google is a remarkable tool for research.

It is also a dynamic tool that changes frequently.

Right now, the top slots in a Google search get there by spending money and time. Search engine optimization is tricky, but what you need to know is – the top spots on a Google search belong to savvy marketers who invest time and money.

If you are selling a product – let's say, a JV proposal eBook – you can use Google to identify who the strongest marketers are in your niche.

I just did a search on "JV proposal," and eBook. There were almost 8,000 hits.

Find the ones that resonate with your niche, subscribe to their ezines, and read them.

People with big lists publish ezines and newsletters.

If you're selling an eBook about Search Engine Optimization, do a search on "Search Engine Optimization" and see where that leads.

Today, it turns up over seven million "hits." That's more than we need.

It also turns up a lot of information – if somebody gets to the top of a list that big, they're worth talking to.

If you've got the Google toolbar, or the Alexa toolbar, you can find out a lot more about them – but the fact that they turn up at the top of the list tells you just about all you need to know.

Let's look at the obvious resources first.

The best place to look for JV partners is in the world of ezine publishing.

Again, a Google search on "SEO, Search Engine Optimization, ezine" will turn up 229,000 Web addresses.

You should probably start with the top ten. If they're on page 1 of a Google search that is that broad, they've got a lot of traffic. They probably have a large list of subscribers, too.

Read their 'zines. Are their customers your potential customers?

If it's not a perfect match, don't bother.

CHAPTER 38

THE BIG DOGS

The Big Dogs – This is the group that hasn't quite hit "Elvis" status yet, but they're in the trenches and have a good track record. They're easier to get to. You probably don't know their names, yet, but they're easy to find.

You'll see them mentioned in forums. You'll read about them in newsletters. They'll show up as co-authors on books they write with the gorillas.

By the way, the absolute best forum for learning about info-product marketing is Info Product U, at *http://www.InfoProductU.com*. Bill Hibbler and I run that one, and there are hundreds of potential JV partners who are also members.

Find these people while they're still on their way up, and establish a relationship with them.

You might hire them as a coach. You can sign up for my coaching program at *http://www.PatOBryan.com/mentor.htm*.

Subscribe to their ezines and newsletters. Mine are at:

Milagro World: *http://www.MilagroWorld.com*

Effortless eBooks: *http://www.EffortlessE-Books.com*

Effortless Copywriting: *http://www.EffortlessCopywriting.com*

Blog: *http://www.PatOBryan.com/blog.htm*

This business, like every other business, is built on relationships. If you can establish a relationship with a "big dog" before he becomes an "800-pound gorilla," you might end up with a relationship with a real heavy hitter.

CHAPTER 39

EVERYBODY ELSE

Everybody Else – I have hundreds of affiliates for some of my eBooks. About five of them actually make sales. You will naturally attract these affiliates through the ClickBank directory, and through the promotion you get from the other two categories. It might be worth your time to place an ad at *www.CommissionJunction.com*, but I'd make that a low priority at first.

I subscribe to several forums. Most of them have a place where you can advertise your affiliate programs. Be sure to only advertise them in the specific place where they're welcome. If you solicit for affiliates in an informational thread on a forum, you'll get flamed – at best, and banned at worst.

I just did a search on affiliate directories – here are the top ones. Some of them charge to list your product, some don't. I don't have any recommendations. I've found all of my affiliates by listing my products in the ClickBank directory and through personal relationships.

http://www.CommissionJunction.com

http://www.AssociatePrograms.com/

http://www.AffiliateTip.com/

http://www.Affiliate-Programs-Directory.com/

http://www.AffiliateFirst.com/

http://www.Refer-It.com/

CHAPTER 40

WHAT ABOUT THE COMPETITION?

There is no such thing.

A competitor is a potential partner.

A competitor is a person who is already marketing to your customers. They've already got a list of people who buy products like yours.

A list of people "who buy" is much more valuable than a list of people "who are interested in." It takes a leap of faith on the part of the customer to actually reach in their wallet, pull out their credit card, and buy. Once that faith is established, it's much easier to get them to pull out the card a second time.

This is why you are willing to give up a large percentage of the first sale to get names on your list, and this is why your competitors are your best potential partners.

Your potential partner understands this. They also understand that if their customer bought one product in this category, they will probably buy another. They've already got the list. They are looking for products to sell to their list.

It's a win-win proposition.

At an Internet marketing seminar last year, I heard a list owner talk about "creaming" somebody else's list. It made perfect sense. If a list owner sends 10,000 emails directing his subscribers to your sales page, and 1,000 of them buy, then the 1,000 that bought are the "cream" of his list. They are the ones who are interested in your product, and willing to pay for it.

Those are the ones you want.

CHAPTER 41

SAMPLE JOINT VENTURE LETTER

Below is a sample joint venture proposal.

Dr. Joe Vitale said, "It's pretty bare bones, but it will work."

That's what I was going for.

It is just a simple template. Do not copy it verbatim. Use it as a guide.

All the pieces are there. Make your JV proposal as long and as detailed as it has to be, but not any longer.

There is a temptation to include your resume, or detailed information about yourself. Resist it.

Emphasize the benefits of your product, and the "fit" with the list owner's list.

The phrase I hear most marketers use is "polite and persistent." You may not get a response to your first email.

Wait a few days, and then follow it up with a "did you get my previous email" email.

If that doesn't generate a response, wait a few days and then inquire again, including a reminder of the product's benefits and the fit with their list.

111

Dear _____,

Thank you for providing such a valuable resource.

I'm a subscriber to your ezine, _____, and especially enjoyed the issue about _____.

I have developed a new product (written an eBook, developed a software program, etc.) that I think your readers will enjoy and profit from.

The features that make it especially attractive to your subscribers are _____.

It's the _____.

Your complementary copy is at www.____.com

The sales page is at www.____.com.

You are welcome to 75% of the gross sales generated from your list. For the next week, I am offering it to you exclusively, and will not offer it to any other marketer until I have heard from you.

If you are interested in offering it to your list, contact me any time at ____@____.com, 555-555-5555.

Thank you,

_____

CHAPTER 42

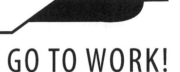

GO TO WORK!

Generating JV relationships, like much else in life, is something you'll get better at as you go along.

Over time, you'll be able to launch a JV deal with a personal email or a casual conversation over lunch.

You've now got the tools to establish those relationships. The sooner you get started, the sooner you'll get there.

CHAPTER 43

SEO FOR BEGINNERS
SEARCH ENGINE OPTIMIZATION
STEP-BY-STEP

Think of this as a "bonus" chapter.

In my opinion, until you've mastered list building, relationship marketing, and product development, everything else is a distraction.

There are people doing some good work in search engine manipulation, AdWords, and AdSense. Joel Comm's work is a good place to start. This chapter gives you a good broad overview of techniques to get your web page indexed by the search engines, and some good ideas for driving traffic to your site.

Once you've mastered the basics, this is your next step.

CHAPTER 44

INTRODUCTION: WHAT IS SEARCH ENGINE OPTIMIZATION?

What if you threw a party and nobody came? That's what can happen if you don't optimize your website so that it is search engine friendly.

Launching a website IS like throwing a party. It should be an event. The reasons events often fail is because:

- **The guests (your customers) never received an invitation to your launch in the first place. This happens when you fail to list your website's URL properly in search engines.**

- **Your customers can't find the address of the party. This can happen when you decide to go the cheap route and opt for a free hosted domain instead of your own domain name.**

- **They have found the address but are greeted with a sign that says "Party Cancelled." This would be the famous 404 message that you often see on the Internet that informs you that a site has mysteriously disappeared or been removed.**

- **A bad rumor has gotten around that your party (website)**

117

is boring and you can't deliver what you promised on the invitation. Your email is sent into a void, your chat forum doesn't work, and people associate your good website name with slow service and copious email offers.

To put it succinctly, search engine optimization is the process of making your website as identifiable as possible. A website that is not properly search engine optimized is simply floating in cyberspace, kind of like an abandoned space ship.

Keep in mind that having a people-friendly website is not the same as having a search engine friendly website. A search engine friendly website is one that appeals to tiny robots called "spiders" that search the World Wide Web for your site every time someone types in a search for information.

In this chapter, we are going to take you through the basics of how to create a search engine friendly site, including how to create a search engine friendly web page, how to submit your URL to the search engines and how to optimize your site using search engine friendly content. We are going to teach you how to talk to robots!

Talking to robots is not as hard as it sounds. It means knowing a bit about HTML and keyword optimization. It entails knowing how to phrase things so that computers understand the language of what it is you are trying to convey or sell when you submit your site to the search engines. Also, search engine optimization is not as technical as it sounds. To some extent it also involves using your intuition to second-guess what your customers might be looking for every time they use a search engine such as Google or Yahoo! to search for a product.

The reason it is so important for you to know how to talk to robots is because it is an aspect of website and e-commerce marketing that is vital to the branding and marketing of your product or service. By doing just a few simple things, you can give your website an edge over the competition's by making your business recognizable to both spiders and potential visitors alike.

CHAPTER 45
PART I. CREATING A SEARCH ENGINE FRIENDLY WEB PAGE

1. Finding the Perfect Host

Your first step to preparing yourself for search engine optimization is to make sure that you have a website that is functional. Having a site that works seamlessly to provide customers with a gratifying experience (as opposed to a disappointing one) is your best form of advertising and marketing.

Your choice of website host is important because a site that is down half the time is not customer or search engine robot friendly. You can advertise your site all you want but if your site is not a stable entity in cyberspace, then you are simply shoveling all of your time and effort into a black hole. This is why it is absolutely crucial to find a web host that keeps its promise to keep your site running 24 hours a day; seven days a week.

Some hosting companies provide 'free hosting' which is a fine solution if you want to share news of how your granny's garden is doing lately, but not so fine if you wish to present a professional image on the Internet. Many people have enrolled in free hosting only to find that when it comes time to optimize their site that visitors are not directed to their page but rather to a page that advertises their web hosting services.

Anybody can sell you space on a server. Some hosting companies behave like grifters. They will sell you a space that is the virtual equivalent of a condemned building, and then they will refuse to cancel your payments or refund your money when your business can't thrive in it.

So, practice the principle of "Buyer Beware." Make sure your website host promises you the stability you need to stay in business. Otherwise your customers may be led to a disappointing experience that brands you as a lousy vendor for life.

2. *How Free Hosting Can Cost You*

Would you build a house on quicksand? That's what you would be doing by refusing to invest even a little bit of money in a website host. The host you choose should provide your business with a strong foundation on which can you build in the future.

Basically there are two kinds of hosting:

☐ **Shared hosting.** This means that your website will be sharing space with a number of other sites. The host manages the service, but it is your responsibility to maintain your site and your account. The major drawback is that if one of your server neighbors gets heavy traffic, your site's performance might be compromised as your portal accommodates all of the unexpected guests.

☐ **Dedicated hosting.** In this scenario, you lease a server from a host. You'll pay more, but because you're not sharing traffic with others, you don't have to worry about your site suddenly appearing to degrade or disappearing from cyberspace altogether. This option is sometimes divided into **unmanaged hosting**, which provides limited support for lower fees, and **managed hosting**, which costs more but provides higher-level support, maintenance, security and services.

Free hosting is only recommended to you if you don't have a cent to your name. However, free web hosting has some MAJOR disadvantages, especially when it comes to search engine optimization that I should mention here:

POP-UP ADVERTISING

Search engine spiders and robots dislike pop-up advertising. Free web hosts use pop-up advertising to cover the costs of providing your site the free web space and associated services. Some hosts require you to place a banner on your pages; others display a window that pops up every time a page on your site loads, while still others impose an advertising frame on your site.

Pop up frames are not recommended as they may cause problems when you submit your website to search engines. Search engines HATE pop-ups, especially the big ones like Overture, Google and Yahoo!. Often pop-ups and pop-under advertising is read as empty space by search engine spiders! This means that the robots will simply ignore your site rather than list it in their directories.

Also, if you are planning to exchange links with another site or become part of a multilevel program such as ClickBank, you may not be allowed to join. This is because a pop-up or pop-under cannot be backspaced to the previous page.

This is irritating to your customers and most free web servers have a very bad habit of adding more free advertising as your site grows older. This is part of a big hint to stop you from freeloading and purchase their space.

LOUSY DOMAIN NAMES

Free websites usually offer you what is called a split domain name. You are much better off to have your own domain name. An example of an owned domain name would *www.TreasureChest.com*. If you choose a free hosting service your domain might change to look something like – *www. FreeSiteHosting.com/treasurechest*.

When people search for your site they will probably be led to a page that advertises FreeSiteHosting.com (my mythical hosting company) rather than your site. Then they will have to search for your site within the free server. You can lose a lot of potential business after they give up trying to enter your business name into yet another search engine in a futile attempt to find you.

LOUSY SEARCH ENGINE PRESENCE

Also when you try to enter a split domain name into a URL submission service anything after a slash tends to be cut off. So let's say for example that you decide to enter *www.FreeSiteHosting.com/treasurechest* into a search engine submission tool. The next thing you know, when your site is listed in the search engines, your full domain name is there, but when you click on it, it leads you to some strange portal or information about how to register a domain name with your host. Even worse it sometimes tells others that your domain name is for sale! Then after a year or so passes, a complete stranger may try to sell your own business name back to you!

LACK OF BANDWIDTH

Free and cheap web hosts impose a limit on the amount of traffic your website can receive per day and per month. This means that if your site attracts visitors beyond a quota that is based on what you are allowed in terms of traffic during a certain time period, the web host will disable your website (or perhaps sends you a bill for the hosting of the excess traffic).

It is difficult to recommend a specific minimum amount of bandwidth, since it depends on how you design your site, your target audience, and the number of visitors you expect to attract to your site. In general, 100MB traffic per month is too little for anything other than your personal home page.

CHAPTER 46

CHOOSING A COMMERCIAL WEB HOST

s mentioned before, the more stable your site is, the easier it is to search engine optimize your Internet business. Here are some things to look for when choosing a website host:

SPEED AND RELIABILITY

Look for statistics somewhere on the web host's website that describe something called minimum uptime. This figure describes the percentage of time that your website will actually be ONLINE. This figure should 99.5% or higher! If they don't provide this kind of information upfront, then it is an indication that the site might suffer from a lot of downtime. This not only costs you time and customers, such a site is not even worth search engine optimization.

PLENTY OF BANDWIDTH

Bandwidth (sometimes loosely referred to as "traffic") is the amount of bytes that are transferred from your site to visitors when they browse your site per day.

Don't believe any commercial web host that advertises "unlimited bandwidth." The host has to pay for the use of the bandwidth, and if you consume a lot of it, most will simply just charge you more. Many startup sites that require high bandwidth have found this out the hard way when they suddenly receive a lot of hits.

The reason this is important is because your website can actually start to cost you if your search engine optimization techniques are working and you receive a lot of hits.

To give you a rough idea of the typical traffic requirements of a website, most new sites that are not software archives use less than 3GB of bandwidth per month. Your traffic requirements will grow over time as your site becomes more well-known. CHECK THE FINE PRINT of the web host's Terms of Agreement policy to see if they will charge you any extra if your site uses too much bandwidth.

SUBDOMAINS

The best free hosting services do not charge you extra for adding anywhere from ten to twenty subdomains. For those of you not familiar with subdomains, it allows you to customize a page and give it a different URL. This can be useful when it comes to adding search engine optimized content to your site.

For instance, let's just say that you are the owner of *www.TreasureChests. com*. However an individual from another site has sent you an excellent article about pearls that is brilliantly optimized with searchable keywords and you want to post it on your website so that it can draw more traffic to your site. In this case you would want to create a page called. *www. TreasureChests.com/pearls*.

2. *What's in a Domain Name?*

There are a number of sound business reasons as to WHY you should own your own domain name:

- If you ever change your web host, your domain name goes with you. Your regular visitors or customers who knew your site name as *www.TheRightStuff.com* (for example) would not have to be informed about a change of URL. They would simply type your domain name and be redirected to your new site. This is important because the last thing you want to do is redo all of your search engine optimization all over again if you have to move your site!

- If you are a business, a domain name gives you credibility. Few people would be willing to do business with a company with a dubious URL like *http://www.AngelOfFire.com/pearls-treasurechest/70896/htm*

- If you get a domain name that describes your company's business or name, people can remember the name easily and can return to your site without having to look it up or search all over the Internet. In fact, if you get a good name that describes your product or service, you might even get people who were trying their luck by typing your product in their browser.

- If you want to attract sponsors, link partners or advertisers to your website, owning your own domain name gives your website credibility and respectability.

If you can, I highly recommend that you attempt to make your domain name identical to your website name. Although this is not always possible, try to register a domain that at least closely mimics the website you are creating.

For instance, let's just say you want to open an online new age bookstore and call it NewAgeBooks.com. Alas, you will see that domain is taken and someone else on a site called WhosIt.com is offering it for sale for $4,000. WhosIt.com is a search engine that allows you to find out who owns what domain name and how much they want to charge you to own it.

As your site specializes in selling books about new age things, you then decide to call your site NewAgeBooksOnline.com. However when you try to buy *www.NewAge-BooksOnline.com*, you find out somebody else has taken it. However, you do see that newageBooks.net is available to buy for $10, so you purchase that and newageBooks.net becomes the name of your site.

Naming a site after its domain name is important because it is part of what marketers call branding. If your website name is also part of your URL, they'll automatically know where to go and what to type into a search engine to find you.

Imagine that your business is called NewAgeBooks.net but somebody else holds the domain name of NewAgeBooks.com. What happens if a customer types "new age books" into a search engine? Chances are they'd wind up at your competitor's website. Studies show that people remember dot com more than dot net. This is why I recommend that you keep your domain as simple as possible and identical to the name of your website. Also whenever possible, try to get the .com as that is what people remember more than .net, .info, .biz or any of the other domain name suffixes.

In the modern world of the Internet, where people automatically turn to the Web for information, it *pays* to have a domain name that reflects your site or business.

On the other hand, if you're just starting out, you might prefer the cheaper alternative of trying to obtain a domain name first, and then naming your website (or business) after the domain that you were offered. So if you've acquired, say, the domain name "newageBooks.net", then consider naming both the title of your website and your URL newagesbook.net. This is much better than naming it as something more abstract as The Bookstore for Aquarian Children in the New Age. Keeping the two consistent simply makes it easier for the search engines to find.

I know that a number of people seem to think that your domain name really must be some generic name like "Typewriters.com" if you are selling typewriters, but seriously, if you were looking for a typewriter, you'll probably already have some brands in mind, and you're more like to try out things like RemingtonTypewriters.com or AntiqueTypewriters.com rather than just Typewriters.com.

Domain names can be of any length up to 67 characters. You don't have to settle for an obscure acronym for a domain name like FMA.com when what you mean is FreeMarriageAdvice.com.

However nobody seems to really be sure whether a long or short domain name is better. Some marketing experts argue that shorter domain names are easier to remember, easier to type and far less susceptible to spelling mistakes: for example, "RelationshipHelp.com" is easier to remember and less prone to typos than "RelationshipTherapistsOnline.com." If possible try to relate it to a keyword.

Others argue that a longer domain name is usually easier on the human memory – for example, "GTN.com" is a sequence of unrelated letters that is difficult to remember and type correctly, whereas if we expand it to its long form "GetTherapyNow.com", clients are more likely to remember the domain name.

A site that contains the words "marriage advice," "therapy" or "free" might fare better in the search engines than a site that is simply an acronym such as FMW.com

My advice is to go for a shorter name as long as it is very to the point and meaningful. If it is longer than two words, then make sure it is a phrase or a combination of keywords that people who are searching for you might be likely to type into a search engine.

PLURALS, "THE", AND "MY" FORMS OF THE DOMAIN NAME

Very often, if you can't get the domain name you want, the domain name registrar will suggest alternates for you to choose from. For example, if you wanted TreasureChest.com, and it was taken (and of course it is), the domain registrar will suggest other options such as:

TheTreasureChest.com

MyTreasureChest.com

TreasureChests.com

If do decide you take the "the..." and "my..." forms of the domain name, you must always remember to promote your site with the full form of the name as this is another good way for you to accidentally drive traffic to the lucky owner of plain old TreasureChest.com.

If you can't get the ".com" domain of their choice, but find the ".net", ".org" or other country-specific top-level domains (TLDs) available (like .de, .ca, .nu, .uk) should you go for it?

This depends on largely on the nature of your business. For instance if you are a local historian who is based in New York and specializes in documenting the history of the city, it is not a bad idea to use the domain associated with that city if it is available. Example: NewYorkHistory.ny

However, avoid country or city specific URL's if you want to attract a global audience (".net" and ".org" extensions are actually quite acceptable domain names. For some, the ".org" extension actually describes the non-profit nature of their organization.)

Others would say to not compromise when it comes to the ".com" issue. As grounds for their arguments, they cite that some browsers, such as Overture, work alphabetically. Apparently, the browser searches for a domain name "AAAAutomotive.com" before attempting "Automotive.net", As such, people who do that will be delivered to your competitor's site if you do not also own the ".com" extension.

CHAPTER 47
HOW TO REGISTER A DOMAIN NAME

Almost everywhere there is web hosting there is a domain name registration system. They give you permission to use the name you want by submitting for approval to an organization called InterNIC.

For example, if you choose a name like Treasure-Chest.com", you will have to go to a registrar and pay a registration fee. Usually the fee ranges from $15 to $35 for that name. That will give you the right to the name for a year, and you will have to renew it annually for (usually) the same amount per annum.

Some commercial web hosts will register it and pay for the domain name for free (usually only the commercial web hosts), as long as you agree to sign up for a minimum of a few years of web hosting.

Step-By-Step Instructions

If you want to register a domain name, here's what you need to do:

First of all, milk your imagination and try to think of a few good domain names that you'd like to use. Murphy's Law dictates the one that you want is already taken, so try to come up with a few variations on your theme. For instance if you are after the website *www.PrettyThings.com* also consider options such as *www.MyPrettyThings.com*, *www.BeautifulThings.com*, *www.PrettyObjects.com*, *www.PrettyThing.com* and whatever else you can think of that is thematic to what you want to sell!

Get your credit card or PayPal account ready to pay a maximum of $50 or so for a domain name. This is a requirement of most if not all registrars. It will allow you to claim and get the domain name immediately on application.

If you have not yet decided on a web host but want to hurry up and register your domain name before somebody else does, you can always register the domain name separately and then host later. This way you can quickly secure your domain name before it's too late and still take your time to set up the other aspects of your site. Some of those registrars also provide you with a free email address at your own domain name, like *Sales@TreasureChests.com*.

CHAPTER 48

PART II. USING SEO CONTENT TO CREATE A WEB PRESENCE

1. What's in a Title?

ost writers know the selling points of an informative or witty title, but writing titles for web pages and for selling web pages is very different than writing titles for normal advertising. As a beginning web author, you need to realize that you will be dealing with two types of titles:

1. The in context title. This is the title that sits at the top of your web page.

2. The out of context title. This is the title that is displayed by search engines or in archival pages after a search. It usually appears onscreen as a fragment and as part as a long sorted list. If you neglect to come up with a robot-friendly out of context title for your web pages, many search engines will simply display your title as "Home Page" or "New Page 1". This does not exactly entice customers to visit your site!

The in context title is the title that is featured on your ACTUAL home page. Let's just say you have the title "The World's Shiniest Diamonds" home page. This page displays your logo, a picture and a description of your product that actually relates to your URL, which may be quite different as in TreasureChest.com. The purpose of your site is obvious to the reader.

However when you write an out of context title, you need to keep in mind that it is for the benefit of the search engine robots that spider the Internet whenever anyone searches for diamonds. You can't rely on graphics or anything else to entice search engine robots to your site. All they are going to see is a phrase that has to concisely and distinctively express the essence of your product in just a few words. Unlike the in context title, the out of context title has to carry the full weight of describing the page's contents.

The World's Shiniest Diamonds may not cut it as an out of context title as people do not tend to search the word shiny or world when looking for diamonds. A good out of context title for such as site would "Cheap Lab Created Diamonds" as they are more likely to search with such terms as "cheap" or "lab created" when they are trying to find you!

2. *The Art of the Blurb*

If you examine the best websites, you will notice that most of them are written in blurb form. The blurb form jam-packs as much info as possible into the shortest space possible. This is because reading a long rambling essay on the Internet is not only hard on the eyes, but it also isn't punchy enough to sell products any more.

There are also two kinds of blurbs: the in context blurb that is found on a page in your site and the out of context blurb that is submitted to search engines.

An in context blurb that is written on a web page is ideally about 600 words long, never shorter than 250 words and never longer than about 900.

An out of context blurb is about 250 words long and appears as a short description of what your site is about on a search engine. It functions as a short but concise summary of the entire contents of your web document.

Both your in context and out of context blurbs should be loaded with keywords (you can find a list of search engine optimization tools in the third section of this book.) Charging your content with keywords is essentially what search engine optimized content is!

3. *Writing Search Engine Optimized Content*

The truest search engine content is content that is created using keywords or keyphrases. These words and phrases are the terms that are most commonly entered into search engines when consumers perform a search on your product or service. You want to write ALL of your content, including titles, the body of your web pages, and all out of context material using the most popular keywords so that your customers can easily find you on the net.

The keywords that you use for your page title may also determine whether or not a user will want to view your URL. The out of context page title usually has two parts: a keyword or keyphrase that is friendly to the search engine and phrases that distinguish your page from the thousands of listings that use the same title.

Keep in mind that the first part of the title's intention is to improve your search engine ranking and the second part's intention is to increase the click through rate of your pages once they rank well on the search engines. This is where knowledge of your target market becomes crucial!

4. *How to Choose the Right Keywords*

The first key to using keywords is to avoid using single words as they are way too broad to define your product. Also there are just way too many competitors out there thinking the same thing you are!

Your key to success here is finding the appropriate "niche" keywords. You also want to use two or three words strung together, also known as "keyphrases." Studies have shown that most people type in two or three word combinations when they conduct searches, not single words.

Coming up with a list of the most targeted keyphrases for your website involves a bit of brainstorming and utilizing some free online web tools which are discussed in Part III of this book.

One method is to put yourself in the headspace of your site's visitors, and write down words and phrases that you think they would use when searching for a site such as yours.

You can also use a Dictionary and/or a Thesaurus to come up with related or alternate words. If you don't have a hard copy, there are fantastic online versions located at:

http://Thesaurus.Reference.com/

http://Dictionary.Reference.com/

If your imagination fails you, look up your competitors online and see what kind of keywords they are using. It might inspire you to go in the right direction.

If you're trying to target a certain geographic location, make sure to include your city and state in your keyphrase list. This is especially important right now, as many of the search engines have branched out into offering "local search."

5. Use Articles and Information as Traffic Magnets

The more information you have on your site, the more likely your pages are to be crawled by the search engines. When it comes to SEO marketing, all information can be seen as a money magnet.

Any information that you own can be considered assets that can be divided up, repackaged and parceled out to be:

- **Sold as articles**

- **Reprinted as articles with your URL attached to drive traffic to your site**

- **Reprinted in non-virtual sources to drive traffic to your site**

- **Used as free bonuses, tips or advice**

- **Used to stack up your archives with both that "hot" and "timeless" information that will keep your visitors returning to your web pages for more**

- **Used as the basis of a blog.**

No word that you own should go to waste. Material can be rewritten, revised and revamped to create press releases and newsletters.

Once you have written the article, you can use it to generate traffic by emailing it to other publishers or webmasters. Since your article is filled with real, useful information about your topic, many editors will be happy to post the articles on their websites and in their ezines. Also, if you are writing on a topic, what you write about should be naturally keyword optimized.

To get your articles posted, type the topic of your article into the top engines such as Google or Lycos. This should lead you to hundreds of sites that are about your topic. Perform a sub-search using the phrase "submit article" and this should lead you to sites that ask contributors to submit articles.

Submit your articles along with your URL and byline, and watch yourself rapidly turn into a sought over online expert as people then find your SEO content on other people's sites along with that link that leads them to you! This is a great way to increase your traffic, and the repeat visitors should increase your visibility in the search engines.

6. Buying Articles from Syndication Sites

If you are completely talent free, always acquire expert content from syndication sites. Each day, writers for syndication submit thousands of articles for distribution. All the writer wants in return for their "expert" content is a link to their URL.

Here are some of the top sources for finding free, reprintable articles:

First in Articles: *http://www.1st-in-Articles.com/*

Marketing Words: *http://www.MarketingWords.com/articles.html*

Idea Marketers: *http://www.IdeaMarketers.com/*

Market Position Newsletter: *http://www.BizWeb2000.com/articles.htm*

Articles for Reprint: http://www.l1nk.com/urr/twt.html

Constant Content: http://www.Constant-Ccontent.com

7. Pay for Premium Content

You know the old saying, "you get what you pay for." In this case, you will search for the crème de la crème in terms of expert authorship Internet libraries, and then write the author for permission to buy web rights for the article.

You can also contact world-renowned experts at local or distance universities to see if you can acquire the rights to papers and studies that may support the persuasive aspect of selling your product.

Very often you might find this content in a book you have read, in which case you will have to contact the author, the author's agent or the e-publisher to buy rights for the material. If the author is famous it is a real plus, because his name will rank higher in the search engines, and so will your site!

8.   Hire a Ghost Writer

This is a good idea for those who have great ideas but consider themselves to be too busy to master writing search optimized content. There are several main sites on the web where writers place bids on projects posted by people wanting articles, web content, search engine optimized material and eBooks. These are:

- *www.Guru.com*
- *www.eLance.com*
- *www.FreelanceWriting.com*

It seems that most freelance writers on the web have conglomerated in either one or more of these places. You might also consider hiring writers from there.

9. *Get Your Visitors to Supply Your Content*

What better way to generate content and develop a sense of community at the same time than to ask your customers to contribute articles to your site's ezine, forum or newsletter?

You can also get visitor-supplied content by creating a blog (easily done by using a blog template) and by writing short pieces. Then ask your readers to respond with comments. Very often, a blog will attract other individuals who will exchange links with you to increase your traffic. This also helps increase your visibility in the search engines.

This tactic works very well with sites that have a how-to aspect to them such as recipes or gardening. You simply edit the content for style, length and grammar and then toss in a few of your own comments. This material can be posted on your site or sent out as a newsletter.

10. *Make Them Sign a Guestbook*

Nobody should ever leave your site without being asked to sign the guestbook. That is the single most efficient way to garner emails for your database. Also guestbooks offer you important insights as to how your business is going. Sometimes the spiders in search engines also pick up on content in guestbooks, so even if they are not deliberately search engine optimized, they are still helpful when it comes to increasing your web recognition and presence.

11. *Add a Section of Useful Links*

Search engine spiders seem to be friendliest to sites that contain a lot of links. You can mask this as a section of recommended resources or as simply a list of favorite links.

These links can also contain the HTML that leads your customers to your affiliates. It is somewhat classy to also include information that is written by other experts in your field (with whom you have exchanged links with of course) – there is no sense in driving your traffic to your competitor's site by just letting them add their link.

12. *Add a Forum, Blog or Chat Room*

Most web hosts these days, including the ones that offer free hosting and domain names, also provide you with free web tools that you can use to install these three features on your site:

- **A forum – allows you to seed conversations (called threads) that might be the subject of interest or debate to your visitors.**
- **A blog – allows your visitors to voice their opinions in an ezine type format.**
- **A chat room – allows you to interact directly with your customers by holding online seminars or gatherings. It also allows your customers to converse with each other and perhaps meet a kindred spirit.**

Both Bravenet and Homestead are web hosts that are very well known for providing these types of tools to users.

13. Add a "Recommend Your Site" Function

This is a plug-in tool that you can install on your site that is offered by some web hosts. Your visitors click on a button, and a box pops up providing your readers with a form that explains how to recommend your site to five friends. This is one way of getting your customers to do your marketing for you!

14. Install a Search Engine

Several search engines, including GoTo.com, Google and Overture offer a pay-per-click program that allows you to put a search engine on your site. You are paid (usually a couple of cents) each time someone enters a search into your site. In return, the search engine consumes some of your bandwidth by displaying ads to products that are related to your own.

CHAPTER 49

PART III. SUBMITTING YOUR SITE TO THE SEARCH ENGINES

So now you have this fantastic site! You are ready to launch! How do you let everybody know where the party is?

People cannot find you on the web unless you are listed in the search engines. Without that search engine listing, you are simply not on the map!

URL (website address) submission is not that difficult, and you need to be practical about what you can personally achieve as this is not an area that boasts many "short cuts" to success. It can take months to get into the search engines, and years to develop a site that gets top rankings. In fact, search engine ranking can take such a long time that *I highly recommend that you develop a personal plan of action for submitting your URLS the minute you have a domain name, subdomain names and an idea of what your keywords are…!*

1.   *A Simple Plan of Action*

As URL submission can be a complicated process, I have developed a simple plan of action to help you achieve optimum result:

1. **Make sure your site is working properly!** It doesn't matter how many people you attract to your website if, once they get there, they are frustrated by links that don't work, images that don't load and worst of all, a malfunctioning merchant account!

2. **Choose keywords, and incorporate them into the language of your site for the search engines.** Make sure your site is easy for humans to read, but also make sure it is easy for search engine robots to find as well. This involves choosing the right keywords and adjusting your page title, meta tags and first paragraph so that they are showcased in the best possible manner.

3. **Submit to the major search engines.** It only takes about 10 minutes to submit your site to the search engines using the various auto-submission programs that are on the net. Unfortunately it can take three days to six weeks to six months for the major search engines to list your site.

4. **Submit your URL to the major indexes.** Take the time to supply a hand typed, search optimized submission to Yahoo!, Google and Overture. These are probably the three most important places to have your site listed on the Internet, because a listing in these directories can help boost your overall search engine rankings everywhere!

5. **Submit to the general indexes.** There are many less efficient indexes on the Internet that are worth submitting to, too. General indexes fall into a number of categories including country subject specific indexes, international indexes and special purpose indexes. Typing in

your prime keyword plus the word directory or index can help you find which directory is best for your submission.

6. Consider using pay-per-click engines. The good news about listing in search engines and indexes is that it's free. The bad news is that it doesn't bring you targeted traffic. There are, however many search engines, such as Overture.com that provide you with targeted traffic. The idea is that you pay a couple of cents for each click on a targeted keyword.

2. *Determine your Keyphrases*

The easiest way to come up with keyphrases is to ask yourself "What would someone trying to find me type in the little box when they search?" Make a list of what comes to mind and then try them out on the search engines. See if the keyphrases that you are thinking about actually lead you to a service or product that resembles your own… the results are usually unexpected.

If your business is geographically restricted, then your keyphrases should reflect this. For example, if you are a real-estate broker in Toronto, Canada, then the keyphrase "buying real estate" is a waste of time; instead, the more specific phrase "buying real estate in Toronto, Canada" is what you want to be thinking about.

Think about variations on the keyphrases and write them down. Once you use a keyword search engine, it might turn up the following keyword examples:

> **Real estate in Toronto, Canada**
> **Real estate brokers in Toronto, Canada**
> **Buying real estate in Toronto, Canada**

Selling real estate in Toronto, Canada

Renting real estate in Toronto, Canada

Home buying in Toronto, Canada

House buying in Toronto, Canada

Selling a house in Toronto, Canada

House selling in Toronto, Canada

Real estate brokers in Toronto, Canada

Buying real estate in Toronto, Canada

Home buying in Toronto, Canada

House buying in Toronto, Canada

Selling a house in Scarborough, Toronto, Canada

You get the idea. On Overture's search suggestion page, you just type in a very general keyphrase (like "real estate"), and it tells you all of the more specific keyphrases that relate to that keyphrase and how many hits they got. When constructing any copy, you should keep this in mind to enrich your copy with as many keyphrases as possible.

WordTracker is commercial software that you can buy that helps you develop lists of relevant keyphrases, ranked by their popularity. It then queries the major search engines to determine which keyphrases are the least competitive.

Still your best course of action is to use the Overture search engine tool for now because it is free!

3.   *Creating a Title Tag*

At this point, you know what your best keyphrases are. Your next step is to create a search engine friendly title tag.

This is an out of context title, meaning that it has to be good for search engines, not for people. For instance a title such as Donna Jones Toronto Real Estate Broker is not optimized. The most important thing to remember is that: ***All your most important keyphrases should be in the TITLE tag.***

This means that you have to craft your title out of your most important keyphrases and then sandwich them inside an HTML title tag. Also, keep in mind that browsers only display the first few words of a title tag (whatever fits into the title bar of the window). So while the first sentence of your title tag should be "human friendly", the rest can be just a list of keyphrases.

Try to keep the title between 15 and 20 words, but you might want to try longer title tags on some of your pages, just to see what happens! So Donna Jones might have a title that looks like this:

<TITLE>Real Estate in Toronto, Canada- Scarborough Bluff- Buying Selling Houses Homes Apartments Commercial Property Office</TITLE>

The reason for this is that the three most important places to have keyphrases and phrases are your title tag, your meta tags, and your first paragraph. You want them to all contain the same important words; this increases your keyphrase *density* and improves your rankings in the search engines.

4. *Mastering Meta Tags*

Mastering meta tags is crucial because on many search engines, the page title is often cut off and the meta description tag is the only thing that gets displayed.

Meta tags go in the <HEAD> section of the HTML page (the same section as the <TITLE> tag). The meta description tag should contain a short description of the web page. If you think of your web page as a newspaper story, then the title tag (the first part of it anyway, not any keywords you tacked on) is the headline, and the meta description tag is the lead paragraph to the news item. In many search engines, your search results will simply be your title tag followed by your meta description tag, so make sure they work together to explain what's on the page.

This is what the format of a meta description tag looks like:

<META name="description" content="whatever you want to place here">

So, in the example of Donna Jones, we might use:

<META name="description" content="Real Estate in Toronto, Canada- Buying, Selling of Houses, Homes, Apartments, Commercial Property and Office Space">

Try to keep the length of this description between 100 and 200 characters. Remember: the description tag should be written for humans to read. It should **not** be a list of keywords, and should be about 50% longer than your title tag.

The other significant meta tag is the meta keywords tag. When you are looking at a search engine submission form, it will ask you to submit your keyphrases in the order that you think is most appropriate followed by commas.

Don't repeat a keyphrase, and don't repeat any individual word more than 5 times or so. Some search engines may penalize you for repeating the same word too often. The exception is common words like "the", "a", "and" and so on. Most search engines ignore them. Play it safe and try not to repeat yourself.

Some people get confused about whether to use commas between phrases, and whether to capitalize keywords. Some search engines pay attention to the commas and others ignore them. So just use commas as appropriate, but don't waste a character putting a space after the comma. Similarly, just capitalize words as you might expect people to normally use them. Most search engines will ignore the capitalization.

In addition, some search engines are sensitive to the order of keywords. For some search engines, "buying real estate" is not the same as "real estate buying". This means it is a good idea to word your phrases in the way you think most people are going to type them in.

If you find that you have garnered a lot of keyphrases that really are relevant to your site, the best thing to do is build "theme" pages devoted to a particular keyphrase or set of keyphrases. These are called "search optimized articles." However, remember to use the most important keyphrases on your homepage.

Most search engines will restrict your keywords meta-tag length between 200 and 400 characters. Unfortunately, this means you may not be able to include all of your keyphrases in your meta keywords tag even if you don't repeat a word too often. The theme pages concept deals with this also. After paying attention to all of the limitations and referring to the list of keywords you found with a search tool, your sample keywords tags will probably end up looking like this:

<META name="keywords" content="real estate in Toronto, Canada, buying real estate in Toronto, Canada, selling real estate in Scarborough To-

ronto, Canada, real estate broker in Toronto, Canada, Toronto, Canada real estate agent, house broker, apartment broker, home sales, houses for sale ">

5.   *The Keyword Blurb*

Some search engines will ask you for a keyword blurb that expounds upon the elements described in your meta title and meta keyword pages. This short paragraph should also contain keyphrases. However, keep in mind that this part of your search engine submission is written for people, not for machines. This is where you introduce yourself to your visitors, so you want to make a good impression.

Try to put this first paragraph as close to the <BODY> tag as possible. Avoid putting graphics or other HTML in front of your first paragraph. Also, use the <H1> or <H2> tag to create a header that emphasizes your opening sentence. Donna Jones might use the following opening paragraph:

<H2>**Are you interested in buying or selling real estate in Toronto, Canada?**</H2>
My name is Donna Jones, and my specialty is helping clients find the perfect home, apartment or condominium in the beautiful lakeside Scarborough region of Toronto, Canada. Contact me for more information about property in Toronto.

6.   *Submitting To the Big Indexes*

The big indexes such as Yahoo!, Open Directory and About.com are the best places for people to find you. However applying to be listed in them can be a bit of a federal case. Still despite all the red tape, proper submission to these indexes is crucial because there is a pronounced trend towards using "human-edited" indexes in search results. In particular, many of the major search engines are starting to use Open Directory index listings in their search results, making it the second most important place to list your site, right behind Yahoo!'s directory.

Another thing to consider is that the ranking of your site depends on how many other pages link to yours and how essential the search engine thinks these links are. That means that a secondary benefit of getting a link on major indexes is that it can improve your ranking on some search engines. For example, getting your site listed in Yahoo! and Open Directory can seriously boost your page rank on Google.

Before you try to submit to one of the major indexes, please take the time to find and read their submission guidelines, advice and limitations.

Here's how to optimize your listings for all the big indexes:

Yahoo!

It costs $300 a year for directory listing in Yahoo!. Here is another eye-roller for you: it typically takes six to eight weeks for Yahoo! to process your site.

There are three types of Yahoo!; the main (original) Yahoo!; the international Yahoo! sites; and the regional (city) Yahoo! sites. The original site is by far the toughest to get into, so if your site is in, or relates to, a country or region served by one of the other Yahoo! indexes, you should first try to get listed in them first. Once you are accepted by one Yahoo! index usually it is contagious, and you eventually end up getting into them all.

Whatever you do don't try to sneak multiple listings into Yahoo!. By this I mean, don't try to make a free application into a paid category. If they catch you, Yahoo! will ban you for life!

If you wish a listing in the Shopping & Services or Business to Business sections (either main or regional) of Yahoo!, you now must use Yahoo!'s

"Business Express" submission option. You pay $299 ($600 for adult sites) and get a quick yes or no to your application. Once you are accepted keep in mind that you have to come up with the same amount of money every year to remain in the directory. Also to make this more crazy-making, paying money does not guarantee a listing! That is why it is so important that you craft a good submission.

Note that you can still submit non-commercial sites to Yahoo! for free as long as you don't submit them to their Business or Shopping & Services sections of Yahoo!

You can also use Yahoo! Business Express to submit non-commercial sites. Business Express buys you a faster decision from Yahoo!. However if a free submission is properly submitted according to Yahoo!'s guidelines, you should get in anyway (if you want to wait six months!)

In addition, Yahoo! also offers Sponsored Listings from $25 to $300 a month, depending on the listing category. Sponsored listings are rotated randomly at the top of category pages of their search engines. In order to get a sponsored listing, you must first get a listing in Yahoo!, and then you can apply for a sponsored listing in the category your listing is in. You can't use this function to change your listing title or description, by the way; it just helps to improve your ranking

To apply for a sponsored listing visit the Yahoo! category page that contains your listing and click on the "What is a sponsored listing?" link.

Also, don't even THINK about submitting to cranky old Yahoo! if your site is not 100% up and running. That "under construction" page is death on a platter when it comes to submitting to Yahoo!. A site with a clean basic design and lots of good content is more likely to get listed than a site full of bells and whistles.

Whatever you do, do NOT bombard Yahoo! with submissions. If you apply more than once a month, they'll ignore you and your children and your children's children. Another good way to get snubbed by Yahoo! is to submit a site to a regional index that has nothing to do with that region, or isn't really a regionally limited site.

HOW TO APPLY TO YAHOO!

Assuming you are not already listed in the index your first step is to find the category page that best suits your site. At the very bottom of this category page will be a small "Suggest a Site" link. Click on it to get to the site submission page. If there is no "Suggest a Site" link, then the page you are on does not allow listings to be added to it, most likely because it is a very general top-level page. Keep searching until you find your right niche category!

When searching for your niche category, try to find one that reduces your chances of being buried alive by other site listings. This usually means a very specific category.

Follow Yahoo!'s instructions or else! If you try to sneak around their rules, they will get you. Don't try to break the rules by doing things like using numbers or brand names in your descriptions.

This might seem odd too, especially in a business that seems to be all about promoting yourself but Yahoo! will frown on any title and description that reads like promotional ad copy. What Yahoo! wants is a descriptive title and description without any hype (and this includes phrases such as 'the best real estate agent in town" and "unrivalled service"

Also, you improve your chances of acceptance if you can keep your meta tag description to about 15-20 words. You might as well edit it down now before Yahoo! does it for you!

As Yahoo! lists its sites alphabetically, it might also benefit you to choose a name that is among the first five or six letters in the alphabet. If you can come up with a suitable title for your site that starts with A, B or C then use it. For instance, "buy a house" is a better title than "real estate agent" because it starts with a "b" and the word "real" will have you listed at the bottom of the page

THE OPEN DIRECTORY PROJECT

The Open Directory Project is an "Open Source" directory much like Yahoo!, but edited by volunteers. As ODP is now the directory-listing source for many search engines (in particular, Google), it's the place to be seen! A listing in ODP boosts your Google page rank almost as much as a Yahoo! listing does! Better yet, it is free!

Open Directory is different than Yahoo! as it only performs WORD searches not KEY PHRASE searches. So much for your sophisticated keyword embedding techniques. So your description for ODP should avoid pluralized words unless they are likely to be in search queries. On the plus side, Open Directory allows you longer descriptions than on Yahoo!, but the category editor (who is very human in this case) may edit you down.

Like Yahoo!, Open Directory asks that you only submit your homepage URL to the most appropriate category.

How to Apply to the Open Directory Project

Go to the Directory. Type a simple query that is likely to be used by someone searching for the contents of the page you are submitting. For example, if your site is lab diamonds try searches like "cheap lab diamonds" or "quality man made diamonds." Find the category that is most appropriate for your site and then click on submit a site at the bottom of the page. This should bring up the submission form.

The "official" waiting period for Open Directory is 3-6 weeks. If you don't get listed within a reasonable amount of time, a polite email to your category editor might speed the process along.

ABOUT.COM

About.com is a very comprehensive index that combines site listings with reviews and editorial content. An editor or guide runs each category, and they are the individuals you have to appeal to in order for your site to be listed. The easiest way to get their attention is a direct email, as opposed to using the "Feedback" link on the pages.

Tips for Getting into About.com

The guides at About.com are looking for what they call deep links. This may not necessarily be your homepage, but rather an article that you have written from an "expert" point of view.

Your best plan of attack is to:

- **Pick an "about" category that suits your site.**

- **Submit an article that you have written on one of your domain pages.**

- **Offer a link back.** Put a link to their site even before contacting them and say, "I find your site such a great resource that I've listed you in our links page."

Why are you doing all this again? It is because getting listed in these directories can boost your rankings in Google and other search engine directories!

7. *How to Be Ignored by the Search Engines*

Here is a list of the common mistakes that first time URL search engine submitters make. Committing any one of these SEO crimes can get you booted from the system or just get your listing ignored.

- Although it is important to have your most important keyphrases entered more than once, it *is* possible to go overboard. Try to keep repeats of your keyphrases to less than thirteen per submission or a search engine may start to treat you like a spammer.

- Search engines don't like affiliate sites with same or similar content (even with a different site design). This includes most "virtual" sites.

- Mirror sites. Submitting mirror URLs to different categories is also considered spam. Multi-lingual sites are acceptable as long as the URL resolves to the appropriate language.

- Sites that use redirects to another site. Using frames to cloak a real URL is also considered spam under some circumstances, so avoid doing it unless you have no choice.

- Sites whose sole purpose is to drive traffic to affiliate links or sites that contain these types of links.

- Sites without original content.

- Sites that are repeatedly resubmitted (over 5 times) without being accepted.

- Web pages that are built primarily for the search engines and not your target audience, especially machine-generated pages.

- Pages that contain hidden text and hidden links.

- Pages that ramble on and on and say a lot about nothing.

- Sites with numerous, unnecessary host names (i.e. Kitchen.com/spoons, Kitchen.com/forks, Kitchen.com/plates etc.).

- Excessively cross-linking to sites that have nothing to do with the content of the site – stick to specific keywords that relate to your customers.

8. *Free Online Keyword Tools*

Here are the best free keyword tools that you can use to find the keywords that can help you find the right phrases and words to supercharge your website with optimized content.

- *http://www.DigitalPoint.com/tools/suggestion/.* **This is an online keyword suggestion tool that shows you the results of your keyword search from both Overture and an**

independent keyword tracking consultant company called
Wordtracker. It helps you find out how often a phrase is
searched for and get suggestions for alternate words as well.

• *http://Inventory.Overture.com/d/SearchInventory/Suggestion/*.
This search suggestion online tool is offered up by Overture.
Type in your word or phrase and find out how many times
that particular word was searched for last month. It also
lists any related searches that include your term.

• *https://AdWords.Google.com/select/main*? This online tool is a
courtesy "think" gadget developed by Google AdWords. Type
in your phrase and you'll be shown a list of other possibilities.
A slightly modified version of this tool is available at *http://
www.MasteringAdWords.com/resources/Google_tool.asp*

• *http://www.eSpotting.com/PopUps/KeywordGenBox.asp*. This
is a keyword generator that shows how many times your
phrase has been searched for in the previous month.

If you're interested in creating "niche sites" and want to see the top ten
lists and top 50 lists that describe what people are interested in on the Internet check out these:

• **Lycos 50 Daily Report:** *http://50.Lycos.com/*
• **Kanoodle:** *http://Kanoodle.com/spy/*
• **MetaCrawler:** *http://www.MetaCrawler.com/info.metac/searchspy*

These keyword sites can help you decide what is hot, not only in terms of products but also in terms of creating an informational site.

Remember that you want to use the keywords that are used *the most often* by web users. The number of times a term is searched in a month is defined as keyword popularity. The reason you want to use the most popular keywords is to generate the most possible traffic to your web pages.

The tools mentioned can help you determine the potential popularity of your niche keywords. If your keywords are too general and your pages don't have a high ranking in search engines, people typing in the more general keywords arc NEVER going to find your pages. They will find the sites that have those general keywords in their URL.

9. *Five Tips Before You Submit*

Now you've got a decent web page, with good content and meta tags. However before you start entering meta tags into search engines, here are some tips on what to do (and what not to do), to improve your relationship with the search engines:

1. GET YOUR OWN DOMAIN

As I have mentioned before in this book, the main reason for getting your own domain name is that some search engines won't list you unless you do. People are more likely to buy from you if you have your own do-main name. Which looks better to you, *http://www.DonnaJones.com/* or *http://Members.Aol.com/home/page-DonnaJones-RealEstate/05781/*?

2. SUBMIT PAGES WITH LOTS OF LINKS

Many search engines are now ranking web pages that contain a lot of links to other sites higher than those that contain fewer links. This is why it is a good idea to submit your pages with as many links to other sites contained in them as possible. However, make sure these links are related to the content of your pages!

Whenever you find a website that has content similar to yours, email the webmaster and ask for a link, pointing out why it would be appropriate. If he has content on his site useful to your visitors, link to him without even offering to trade links. Link to him, then email him and ask for a link back. This helps drive traffic to your site and increases your popularity in the search engines.

The search engine that values link popularity the most is Google. For many people, the true value of the $299 a year cost of a Yahoo! listing isn't the benefit of receiving click through from Yahoo!, but the boost a Yahoo! listing provides for their rankings on Google.

Open Directory doesn't cost anything, but getting a listing in this respected index can boost your rankings in Google.

3. AVOID USING FLASH

Search engines perceive sites with flash as being "empty spaces." Rather than checking out the content, most search engines just discard the URL. God knows how many people's sites have been rejected because a spider inside a search engine denoted their flash as blank space!

4.   AVOID USING JAVA SCRIPT

If you are using Javascript or CSS in your pages, you probably stuck it at the top of your pages. Remember that search engines tend to rate what they find at the top of pages a bit higher so avoid anything that a search engine considers to be fluff -- and that would be pages and pages of Java enabled script.

A better way to do things is put the Javascript (or CSS) in a separate file, and include it into your pages with a single tag. To avoid this kind of headache however, I advise that you avoid using Javascript at all.

Make Sure Your HTML is correct.

Just because your page is displaying nicely does NOT mean that the code itself doesn't contain errors. Search engines read HTML - not what shows up on you pretty pages. The more perfect your HTML, the more likely a search engine is to rank it higher. This is what I mean when I say that URL submission is all about talking to robots.

The World Wide Web has the potential to contribute significant profits to your business by expanding your market area, providing suppliers information about your current inventory levels, giving customers online access to product catalogs, allowing online purchases, and by simply bringing attention to your company.

However, a website can also be a vampire that sucks your will to live if it is not set up with users in mind, if usage isn't measured correctly, if you are not 100% committed to maintenance of the site or if the site is poorly organized and doesn't attract visitors.

Look before you leap! Plan your website before you spend money and time on search engine optimization!

With a little forethought, knowledge of SEO and imagination, it is possible for anybody, including you, to achieve the presence you need to succeed with a business on the Internet!

ABOUT THE AUTHOR

Pat O'Bryan is the Director of the Milagro Research Institute, CEO of Practical Metaphysics, Inc., author of several popular eBooks, and the creator of the Milagro audio series. His Portable Empire is at *www.PatOBryan.com*. He has co-authored several books with Dr. Joe Vitale, including *The Myth of Passive Income,* and his co-writers include David Garfinkel, Yanik Silver, John Assaraf, Bob Doyle and many others.

Pat has contributed to several successful books, including *Life's Missing Instruction Manual*, by Dr. Joe Vitale, *Meet and Grow Rich*, by Dr. Vitale and Bill Hibbler, *Buying Trances,* by Dr. Joe Vitale, and his story was featured in *The Attractor Factor,* by Dr. Vitale.

His "Your Portable Empire" seminar series has proven very popular, attracting attendees from Holland, New Zealand, Australia, and across the United States. His video production company records the seminars, and distributes them world-wide.

Pat is also a successful recording artist and producer, currently under contract with ZYX Records, Merenberg, Germany. He currently has six CDs available internationally, and tours Europe with his German band annually. A touring musician since age sixteen, Pat has shared stages with

Stevie Ray Vaughan, Eric Johnson, Cheap Trick, ZZ Top, B.B. King, and many other notable musical acts.

His irreverent and hard-hitting blog (*www.PatOBryan.com/blog.htm*) is one of the most widely read in the Internet marketing world.

Pat lives in the Texas hill-country with his domestic partner, Betsy, 24 guitars, and their psychotic cat, Ming.

You can find Pat online at *www.PatOBryan.com*, or contact him at P.O. Box 2272, Wimberley, Texas.

www.patobryan.com/abgbonus1.htm

Printed in the USA
CPSIA information can be obtained
at www.ICGtesting.com
JSHW082208140824
68134JS00014B/495

9 781600 370304